There Is Anointing Powers In Your Hands

<u>There Is Anointing Powers In Your Hands</u>

The Anointing Power of your Hands

Parice C. Parker

There Is Anointing Powers In Your Hands

The Anointing Power of Your hands
Copyright © 2013 by Parice Parker. All rights reserved.

No part of this publication may be reproduced, stored in a retrieval system or transmitted in any way by any means, electronic, mechanical, photocopy, recording or otherwise without the prior permission of the author except as provided by USA copyright law.

Scripture quotations, unless otherwise indicated, are taken from the Holy Bible, King James Version, Cambridge, 1769. Used by permission. All rights reserved.

The opinions expressed by the author are not necessarily those of Fountain of Life Publisher's House.

Published by Fountain of Life Publisher's House

P. O. Box 922612, Norcross, GA 30010
Phone: 404-936-3989
Please Email Manuscripts to: publish@pariceparker.biz
For all book orders including wholesale email: sales@pariceparker.biz
To request author email: author@pariceparker.biz
www.pariceparker.biz

Fountain of Life Publishing House is committed to excellence in the publishing industry. The Company reflects the philosophy established by the founder, based on Psalm 68:11, "The Lord gave the word and great was the company of those who published it."

Book design copyright © 2013 by Parice Parker. All rights reserved.
Cover Design by Parice Parker
Interior design by Phyllis R Brown
Editor: Phyllis R Brown

Published in the United States of America

Copyright Library of Congress: TXu1-287-817
ISBN   978-0-9904441-8-3

Date: March 14, 2015

There Is Anointing Powers In Your Hands

Fountain of Life Publishers House

For book orders or wholesale distribution
Website: www.pariceparker.biz

There Is Anointing Powers In Your Hands

The Anointing Power of your Hands

TABLE OF CONTENTS

Introduction..6

1. Press and Push..9
2. Fighting the battle – Defeating Your Giant..........23
3. The Heart of Your hands Beating at Work............43
4. Spiritual Inflammation...60
5. Praying to the Point of no return.........................73
6. Seven Keys to Prayer..98
7. Getting to know your hands Personality............110
8. Figure out Your Faith..150
9. Allowing the Milk & Honey to Flow 167

    in Your Life

               Parice C Parker

The Anointing Power of your Hands

Introduction

God will bestow strength in your life by lifting up of your hands. Your life will be overfilled with HIS Anointing. Absolutely nothing in this world could exist, that is, no vision could have ever flourished without one laying his or her hands upon it. Whatever it is that you are planning to accomplish, it shall be done in the name of JESUS. You must exercise your faith daily for you to strengthen supernaturally. It all depends on your faith in Him. He wants you to have the best of everything in life. When one tries with all of their heart through the power of God, they are never forsaken. God's word is His promise, so if you stand on His word, His promises will be fulfilled. He promises us a prosperous life, good health, conquering power, wealth, fulfillment, peace, joy, happiness and so on. Believe me, God did not create you to do without! Absolutely not,

There Is Anointing Powers In Your Hands

God said, "The Anointing Powers are in your hands, use them to His fullness." God wants you to lay your hands on the vision He has given you. By your faith, your vision shall speak because faith without works are dead. Lay your hands on it and watch Him work through your hands. Let God Anoint the works of your hands; just lay your hands on it.

Parice C. Parker

<u>There Is Anointing Powers In Your Hands</u>

The Anointing Power of your Hands

I can't keep trying to help people that don't care about helping themselves. The more I try, the harder I fall. It is simply not fair.

~Parice Parker

The Anointing Power of your Hands

CHAPTER 1

Press and Push

Once you begin to desire The Anointing to flow through the tips of your fingers you will do all that is necessary to receive it. You will not allow any sort of excuse to accompany your mind. When you hear God, you will begin to press in a state of no return. The key to this is you must hear Him! We receive instructions when God speaks. As we receive those instructions, our freedom is released as we follow through with them. However, your press is not going to be easy neither is it going to be smooth sailing. Often we

There Is Anointing Powers In Your Hands

want want to quit but we can't. *Philippians 3:14 says, "I press toward the mark for the prize of the high calling of God in Christ Jesus."*

    If you really want The Anointing Powers to work through you, then you are going to have to do something out of your ordinary state of mind. You will not be able to do the ordinary with the work of your hands. Now, it is time for the extraordinary to speak through you. Prove your point to God, do what you need to receive The Anointing. Allow the Anointing to feel the unusual effort of your press. Let the Anointing feel the heart of your press, until The Anointing moves in your life. If you want it then you must put your hands on it, like you have lost your mind. Place them in a position to move forward and see God work through them. God is ready to birth a Fresh Anointing out of you. Just as the woman with the issue of blood that suffered for many years and in many ways. She pressed her way out! This woman realized that if Jesus had all the power many said He had, then she was not prepared to suffer any longer. No one knew what this woman was feeling, the pain and agony. When we think of issues we blow it off as soon as

There Is Anointing Powers In Your Hands

we think about it, but issues are extremely painful. This woman struggled to the point of no return. Her mind was made up to reach Him. Stretch your faith and trust God more, let your faith move your mountains. This woman was not prepared to allow any sort of issue neither blood to stop her from stretching her faith. In many cases, we all have begun to stretch for Jesus and many things have tried to interrupt our stretching effort. Just because things look dim in your life, do not give up. Though many obstacles get in your way, keep on stretching until God brings you out. Often many live in a zone of comfort with their faith, until their faith cannot cause them to be moved.

This woman was full of issues, the bible did not list them all. So many, until it caused trouble and agony to become the way many identified her. Issues was her first description and blood was her last – The Woman with The Issues of Blood. Many did not expect Jesus to bring this woman out, but He did. Her issues were countless, but she did not let them stop her from reaching for Jesus. Once she reached for Him she wanted to touch the Extraordinary Supernatural and she did. She struggled to press and many obstacles she had to

There Is Anointing Powers In Your Hands

press through. You cannot even begin to be broken through until you begin to press. In order to press and push you must be positioned to make a move. You must break out of your old to be birthed in your newness. Your pushing effort must be extraordinary and you will not allow anything to stop you. The only thing that should be on your mind is coming out. I do not know all that you are going through, but I know that Jesus has the power to bring you out. Though many things may try to get in your way, you must press at the point of no return and push your way out. I consider this a Supernatural Birthing because you are ready to do away with the old. Once you feel the Supernatural move on you, then you will expect the extraordinary things to come forth in your life. The truth is that your reality to your dreams is in your press. I know that as I journeyed in my high calling many things tried to hinder me and the enemy had purposed to stop me.

Everything in my life grew to a state of oppression in every way. When I tried to put one foot forward, something else happened, to hold me back. Often times my visions tarried and sometimes I did not have everything I wanted in order to get

There Is Anointing Powers In Your Hands

through one threshold to another, but I had my faith. I simply used the voice of the Lord to keep me in a pressing state. Though you may feel that you do not have everything you need, you have more than enough to make it through. Regardless, do not allow a need to stop you. As you will continue your press, God will bring you out. Just continue to move forward. Push and press your way through. You must move and be prepared to move forward in a pressing position with no pushing tolerance level. It is time that your ordinary pressing state of mind becomes the champions of weight lifters. This press is getting ready to be the most powerful press that is going to break you completely free, from everything that has tried to hinder the works of your hands. I pushed my way because I wanted my prize. Getting to your prize is through your press and you are going to need The Supernatural Pressing Power Pushing through you. You have to get to the mark, then your prize will be waiting there for you. Everything that God has marked in your life will be available as you press; He has a mighty way of causing us to press our way out. We all have a certain mark in our life that God predestined us to reach. While your mother was in her mother's womb, God had already predestined this press to come out of you. Your

There Is Anointing Powers In Your Hands

mark is your unlimited resource to heaven that will be available for you to get your prize. Press your way through as the woman with the issue of blood. In addition, that was her last press she ever had to endeavor, it delivered her out of a life full of agonizing issues. Surely, if The Anointing delivered her then The Anointing has the power to deliver you too.

It is just like being a baby in a mother's womb, when that baby is developed and ready to come out it will press its way out of the womb. Even though that child is entering into a world that is strange, it does not care the baby just wants out. Regardless of the time of day, the occasion or the doctor's reports, that baby is coming when it is ready to come out. So therefore, whenever you are truly ready to come out, you will press and push, until the Anointing Powers of Your Hands will prove that God is The Almighty. Let the Anointing work through you, just lay your hands on it and watch what God is going to do for you.

There was a man known by the name of Doubting Thomas and he too had to learn to stretch his hands forth. *Isaiah 58:9 says, "Then shalt thou*

There Is Anointing Powers In Your Hands

call, and he shall say, answer; thou shall cry, and he shall say, here I am. If thou take away from the midst of thee the yoke, the putting forth of the finger, and speaking vanity."

Thomas did not trust his friend's words or his own eyesight. Thomas realized that his doubt was a yoke that needed to be removed. Many times people will trust the things they can hear or see but God wants our trust in the unseen and the things that have not happened yet. I have learned through the years that the eyes can fool you. I once went into a business deal trusting my eyes as my hopes were lifted. I thought this deal was perfect but it was not. Everything your eyes see is not all that it appears to be. We must be careful of the things we allow our eyes to see and ears to hear - research more until Jesus gives you clarity. There were times that Thomas needed to call upon the Lord, but he doubted Him because he was unsure of his faith. His doubt caused him to be unfaithful to God and continuously made him feel insecure. You must let God know that you truly trust Him. God wants us to trust Him in our best and worst times in life. I know when I have gotten in messed up situations, God always brought me out. In the beginning, I did not

There Is Anointing Powers In Your Hands

trust Him as I should, but the more I cried out to Him the more I grew to trust Him. God knows everything about us. He knows exactly what you are going to have to go through, even before you go through it. Your trails and tribulations will bring you closer to God, just as the woman with the issue of blood. If it had not been for her many agonizing issues then how could she have ever pressed her way into The Anointing? God wants you to reach for Him, until you touch The Anointing. He wants you to press harder towards Him until you feel His presence move through you. The Anointing flowed through her fingertips and removed all her issues. In addition, He always knows how to gain our trust.

Occasionally, we have allowed our voices not to be heard by God all because of a little doubt. I have found that if you do not believe in whatever it is that you want to accomplish then no one else will. Out of the many things I desired to achieve, many did not believe that I could and often times doubt tried to steal my belief. Moreover, I continued to try my best to trust in the Lord. God wants you to believe even when it seemed as though things are not working out. Your way out is determined according your belief and your amount of trust in

There Is Anointing Powers In Your Hands

Him. If you have faith the size of a mustard seed, surely God will remove your mountains. The majority of these are due to the fact most people's faith is in a paralytic state and that will cause conflict of movement. When you are in a paralytic state, regardless of what you want to do or try, you simply will just need a miracle. It will stop your hands from plunging forth into the depths of Jesus. Doubt will stop you from being filled with The Anointing and it will cause you not to press and push. It will be impossible to move forward or just move at all. I tell many do not let the yokes destroy you but allow the powers of God to destroy your yokes. *John 20:27 says, "Then saith he to Thomas, Reach hither thy finger, and behold my hands; and reach hither thy hand, and thrust it into my side: and be not faithless, but believing."*

Thomas moved forward though his yokes of fear and doubt tried to stop him. The Anointing begin to remove his yokes of insecurities once he reached for Jesus. When Thomas touched Jesus' wounds it gave him an incorruptible faith. No man would ever have to convince him again because he touched The Truth for himself. Moreover, after Thomas put his fingers through the wounds of Jesus

There Is Anointing Powers In Your Hands

he said, "My Lord and My God" and then Jesus spoke to Thomas and said, "Blessed are those that haven't seen but believe." At this point, a mustard seed of faith begins to grow in Thomas, until his faith had no more room for doubt.

Jesus wants us to believe before we receive our blessings. Often times, our level of belief is not at the height to cause the level of blessings to be poured into our lives. God wants our trust just because He is God. He wants us to know that He has the power to make things happen, before He make things appear in our lives. Trust in the unseen, believe in the impossibilities and prove your trust more to Him by believing greater in Him. God wants you to trust Him like never before. He wants you to believe in The Anointing. It is All-Powerful and it releases your miracles. God has allowed your dreams to be big. He has given you vision and trusted you with it. God wants you to trust Him for it. Put your hands on it and let God work in you. How is it that God is God if He does not show us in action? God is powerful and He loves to anoint our well doings. He gains more recognition of how powerful He is when He works a miracle in your life. He wants your hands on it, the proof has been

There Is Anointing Powers In Your Hands

written but where is your belief? God wants your belief manifested in Him so that others can see just how powerful He really is. He wants to manifest victory in your life. Let The Anointing take control of you. It will lead you into a life of pure satisfaction. I guarantee that your life will obtain greater worth as He will obtain greater glory through the works of your hands. Many will then say, it only had to be God to cause such a miraculous thing to happen in your life. *John 20:28 says, "And Thomas answered and said unto him, My Lord and my God."*

You do not know the half of what God will do in your life. He will fix every broken-down thing in your life, repair every damaged structure, heal every sickness and lead you into a life of prosperity. His Anointing will prosper you, as it will set you free. I know that every part of your hand has a serving purpose. It is to serve Him Glory. If we never use what God has given us, then how is He going to be recognized as God in our life? All you have to do is reach for Him. Once Thomas felt His presence, He claimed Jesus to be His God and His Lord. When you truly know God, you will praise Him for everything in your life including the work of your

There Is Anointing Powers In Your Hands

hands. However, that is why the work that God has given you must be completed. Surely, you are ready to gain. The question is; are you willing to do everything for your dreams to come true?

    A bricklayer cannot lay one brick without the other until he or she reaches forth with thine own hands to grasp the next brick. Then that particular brick that you are grasping must be placed into perfect position, just hold on to it. The Anointing Power is in your reach; in order to receive it you must lift your hands. In addition, there is grasping power and it lies within the palms of your hands. If you pick up something heavy with your fingertips – it will be hard to hold onto. So therefore, you need to place it within the palm of your hands. Your palm serves a holding purpose and your strength lies within it. It is the part between your fingers and your wrist. It is your holding power. Just remember in order for you to move forward you must place one foot in front of another. When you make one step, God makes two. *Proverbs 3:27 says, "Withhold not good from them to whom it is due, when it is in the power of thine hands."*

There Is Anointing Powers In Your Hands

You must begin to step out on faith in order to settle into your promises. God wants you to reach your dreams, which is why He has given you the vision. Once you reach your dreams, then you will begin to live the life you desire. He shows us things in many different forms to inspire us to move forward in our life. He will let you see what your life could be, if you obey Him. He is the one that has caused your heart to desire this vision, which is why you cannot get it out of your mind. He expects you to believe in Him. In addition, He wants you to lay your hands on it. Hold onto your promises and move forth until you reach your promised land. Every want and heart's desire is there, waiting on you. God wants you to use the power He has given you. The Anointing Powers that are in your hands are designed to get you to your land. A land full of promises to bring your heart's desires to reality. God wants you to reach for higher. It is a blessing to have big desires and to be able to visualize them. It is a privilege and a gift from God because everyone does not have vision. *Matthew 13:17 says, "For verily I say unto you, that many prophets and righteous men have desired to see those things which ye see, and have not seen them; and to hear those things which ye hear, and have not heard them."*

There Is Anointing Powers In Your Hands

Dreams are dreams, but visions speak boldly. You are a special person to God and He wants to instruct you on how to accomplish your vision. He wants you to reach the top and He created you to be more than a conqueror. It is going to be a day to rejoice when your vision speaks boldly to the world that He is All-Powerful. Know that God will grant your heart's desires soon after you lay your hands on it. The Anointing powers are in your hands. Once you lay your hands on it, God will turn your negatives into positives.

The Anointing Power of your Hands

CHAPTER 2

Fighting the Battle Defeating Your Giant

You should not fear any situation because God does not produce fear. When you conclude in your mind that faith is dead without works, then you will begin to exercise your faith – stretching it to the point of no return. *11 Timothy 1:7 says, "For God has not given us the spirit of fear; but of power, of love, and of a sound mind."*

There Is Anointing Powers In Your Hands

Fearing life is not of God. Grow up into a David spirit not allowing a huge giant that is bigger than you to destroy your hope, peace, joy or steal your life promises. Too many have given into fear and never made it to their promised land. God wants his children's hearts to be noticed, through the way we live, the things we do and through the things that we encounter. You can either become a slave to your giants or you can be a powerful champion in the name Jesus. If we continue to walk in fear, then how is it that we are going to show others that God is real? God takes great pleasure in our victories. He is awarded the Glory and then you are awarded the honors. Though we feel the force of the many difficulties that have surfaced in our lives, it does not mean that we should not face them. Facing your giant will end all fears within this area of spiritual growth. Just as the rest of the Israelites, surely, David could have feared but instead as a young boy, David had more courage than the ones that ruled in the army. *1 Samuel 17:42 says, "And when the Philistine looked about and saw David, he disdained him; for he was but a youth, and ruddy, and of fair countenance."*

There Is Anointing Powers In Your Hands

David was not thinking about the gigantic size of Goliath, because his heart was set on the size of his faith he had in God. David's faith was recognized as a child and his belief was beyond words. He had faith like no other and his faith astonished the heart of God. He did not have time to fear because his faith was strong. Regardless of the size of the army, David saw that they were incapable of defeating this giant. As David looked towards the army, he could not find one that was prepared to challenge Goliath. David heard the voice of the giant, but his voice still could not compare to his God. David asked the soldiers that were afraid of Goliath, "Who is he to challenge the armies of the living God?" David had courage because he was a *faith walker*. He had the armies of the living God fighting through Him. *Psalms 27:14 says, "Wait on the Lord: be of good courage, and he shall strengthen thine heart: wait, I say, on the Lord."*

Your strength is in Him. David was one to know of God's mighty strength. He had experienced fighting many battles. I too had this one giant fighting against me. We had a lot of trouble from this building. Oh, it was awful. The roof leaked, we needed flooring, electrical repairs and walls. You

There Is Anointing Powers In Your Hands

name it we needed it. We put a lot of time and effort in this building. Actually, we needed a new building, though at times, we must be tested. Sometimes God wants to see how you are going to handle yourself in certain battles. Our ministry survived many battles as we lived under many pressures. We continued paying the expenses as we repaired the building. This building was our giant. No matter how hard things were we never gave up. God tested our hearts and you never know when He is going to test you. The key to passing the tests is that you be good to everyone at all times. Don't judge, regardless of the circumstances. So therefore, I believed in the entire test through dealing with this experience, we passed. The more effort we put in this building the rougher things got. We had to learn true struggle and then how to give in to the power of God. As we fought, the giant fought back. Our hearts were changed after many experiences took place to cause us to spiritually develop. The more mountains we climbed through faith the greater some of us grew, while others could not hold on any longer. *Genesis 22:17 says, "That in blessings I will bless thee, and in multiplying I will multiply thee as the stars of the heaven, and as the sand which is upon the sea shore; and thy seed shall possess the gate of his enemies."*

Sometimes people just need a break in order for God to bring them through. You never know when God is going to use you to help break someone else free. So many told me, I am going to help you. Others said, God sent me to help you. Then another, you are the one God said for me to help. They all just talked but no action. Some even attempted to help but their eyes could not stay focused on the powers of God. Imagine if every superstar right now would have not met the one person that God worked through, to bless him or her. Think of how many people overlooked someone and as they made it, they wished they had helped. I just left it in the hands of God as I prayed to God to bless them. It is something how people will have what you need but are not willing to help or give. I have had friends that saw my need but they too walked out; members that were not willing because of their busy schedules. I laughed as I cried and prayed, as I was hurt. Often many souls will suffer because of someone else's greed. I always said, "When God bless me out I will not treat people as many have treated me." It is so much better to give than to receive. David was one that was willing to fight this giant and so was I. Allow no giant to threaten you and know that God is fighting your battles. Do not be bothered when people do not stick to what God told them to do for you. Walk on in your faith. Though things are not happening as you want them to, they will. God is working your situation out. Remember everything happens for a purpose and God will reveal to you the reason.

I begin to put my hands on what God had given me. He wanted me to use what I had to continue ministering. Eventually, the building became worthless as we lost it. God knows how to remove the giants out of your life. I use the gifts He has given me and I ministered in song and in books. *Psalms 86:13 says, "For great is thy mercy toward me: and thou hast delivered my soul from the lowest hell."*

God taught me through this one experience, to wait on Him. He expanded my vision and caused me to be more of a *faith walker*.

Just take note of how much God is going to bless you because your heart was positioned to be a

There Is Anointing Powers In Your Hands

blessing. Live this and you will be blessed forever. *Genesis 22:17 says, "That in blessings I will bless thee, and in multiplying I will multiply thee as the stars of the heaven, and as the sand which is upon the sea shore; and thy seed shall possess the gate of his enemies."*

I believe that many forget how they achieved and advanced in life. Every time someone makes it – it is always due to someone else helping him or her. Whether they were noticed or someone gave them a chance with their talents; perhaps their work interested someone to invest in them. As you make it, remember where you came from and be prepared to help someone else to achieve. I have prayed for years that God would use and bless my heart to love more and help others. God simply wants us to bless others that are less fortunate. If you want peace in your life then follow what is in your heart. Be prepared for your giants to cease. Realize that in the putting on of your hands that you serve a living God that has all power. Do not allow anyone to mistreat you and make you feel like you are beneath him or her. We must conclude that anyone serving a living God should be treated with love and respect. Sometimes, God will try you by your heart. Keep

There Is Anointing Powers In Your Hands

your heart clean and pure with God at all times. Do not allow any giant in your life to make you appear less. We serve a God that deserves respect at all times. He judges us on how we treat one another. David loved God too much to allow a giant to overpower the God that lived in him. God is powerful and He deserves better than most people give Him. During your battles, your life will show who's in control. Can you relate to how David felt when he said, "Who does that giant think he is compared to my God?" We serve a living God with all power. As we stand up to our many giants, God will give us greater wisdom and vision. Through your courage, you will gain more strength as you continue to stand. God will also flourish your vision. Again, man looks on the outer appearance but God knows what is on the inside of you. David was one that gave God great respect during his battle with the giant. We must look at the giant and say, "Who is he to challenge the armies of the living God?" He was a mighty blessing to his army as he defeated Goliath. Not only did he win but look at all the souls that were saved because he was a *faith walker*. The more you defeat your giants the more your children will possess the gates of their enemies. Every time you win, you will be able to testify of yet another

There Is Anointing Powers In Your Hands

victory. The more victories you win in life the more strength in Him you will have. You must continue in your faith. Many will be delivered from their giants as you continue. Fight with an expectancy to win. However, you will be bruised and wounded but fight to the end. Use your faith to anoint your situation. Allow your faith to move God, so therefore you will not have to work so hard. I was stripped in many battles to man but God clothed me in His Armor. Just as David I could not live by the things my eyes saw, I lived by faith. If faith were not so, I would have died. Faith has caused many to survive. With faith, you will have victory at all times. *11 Timothy 1:7 says, "For God hath not given us the spirit of fear; but of power, and of love, and of a sound mind."*

Your battles are to strengthen you and to spiritually develop you. Help others in the time of their needs. Bless others as God has blessed you. Let others see the power of God in you and show them the power of love. Let your heart be prepared to help others with the love of God beating in your heart. God does not intend you to be fearful in any situation. When you are His, there are no incidents or accidents. God knows how to make things happen

There Is Anointing Powers In Your Hands

in your life. However, we make many mistakes but God makes absolutely none. As He put His claims on you, everything that has happened in your life was meant to be. Some are to strengthen you, while others will make you wiser and give you courage. This battle will bring you closer to His light. In addition, it will awaken you more. As David was preparing to battle he was also preparing to win. He knew God was more powerful than Goliath and before he fought, he knew the battle was already won. Know that you are a winner because God is fighting your battles, as the anointing will be in you.

When you are in the hands of God where does fear fit in? The power of the anointed is awesome in works. *Hebrew 10:31 says, "It is a fearful thing to fall into the hands of the living God."*

God will touch any giant in your life and cause them to be permanently removed without question. Only the Powers of God can beat your giants down. David knew that He was in the hand of His living God so fear could not enter his heart. A giant to David was not a threat or any other detail. David looked at Goliath as nothing compared to his God. He kept in mind the power of the living God

There Is Anointing Powers In Your Hands

He served. I know something miraculous has occurred in your life. You knew it was only God. Just like myself, I had to experience falling into the hands of God. After I woke up and I realized that I was in the hand of God. That giant could not make me fret because God made me move. *Proverbs 8:22 says, "The Lord possessed me in the beginning of his way, before his works of old."*

One time or another you have conquered something bigger than you in your life and only God was able to receive that glory. You knew within your heart that it was not you but it was because of the powers of God that caused hope to rise up in you. That is the exact hope that you need right now in order to gain the victory of winning this battle. David remembered his previous victories that he had won. When he killed the lion and smote the bear with the anointing power that was in his hands. David admired the powers that God had placed within his hands. He knew it was all through the anointing. He knew it was the powers of his living God, fighting through him. *Proverbs 3:26 says, "For the LORD shall be thy confidence, and shall keep thy foot from being taken."*

There Is Anointing Powers In Your Hands

Perhaps you are in a losing state in your life through your battles. In addition, your giants are defeating you; remember that it can all change through your faith. I know that the power of God can turn it around for you. Though your battle seems impossible, know that God has given your hands the power. People fail in life due to their negligence in listening to God. Nevertheless, we can hear Him but the question is do we listen. God wants your heart, mind, body and soul to be pure well as your hands to be cleansed. Eventually it all will work out even though the enemy wants it to work out for his benefit. Always believe that God can use and change every heart. He surely changed me. Know that you are in His hands at all times. JEHOVAH will take care of you just as He took care of David. Not only will He take good care of you He will cover all that is around you. When He took care of David, God also covered the Israelites. That is why it is so valuable to be amongst the people that are covered by the hands of God, it will save your life. God has the power to cover a whole army, so there is no need for you to be worried. *Deuteronomy 33:3 says, "Yea, he loved the people; all His saints are in thy hand; and they sat down at thy feet; everyone shall receive of thy words."*

There Is Anointing Powers In Your Hands

Whenever God is in full control then what is there to fear? You must realize that you are in the hands of the Almighty. You should never fear because God is working in your life. As long as you are in God's hands then fear should not be an obstacle. God has all power in His hands and as long as He is your covering then know you are going to win this battle. Because you are setting in the palm of His hands nothing can or no one will hurt you? Do not allow fear to stop the *Anointing* to move over the works of your hands. *Matthew 11:29 says, "Take my yoke upon you, and learn of me; for I am meek and lowly in heart: and ye shall find rest."*

Once you begin to place the yokes of Jesus around your neck, then you will begin to grow in the power of God. You will gain the anointing power that will loose many to freedom. You will be very compassionate, never looking at any man's down fall. You will begin to pray for them and your heart will feel love that it has never felt. Your spirit will become meek and humble because now you will begin to understand Christianity. You will know its purpose and definition is love. You will walk by faith and be known to many as a *faith walker.* II

There Is Anointing Powers In Your Hands

Corinthians 5:7 says, "(For we walk by faith, not by sight:)."

Regardless of where you are, many will not only see that you are a peculiar person but they will feel you as you speak, walk, move, and pray. You will not need to be introduced because The Spirit of Jesus will be in you. As they look upon you, they will receive power, just by seeing your faith. Jesus is telling you to take His yoke, learn of Him. He wants you to come on your own free will and get it. Though you must suffer as He did, go through as He did you will also rise up as He did. Surely, many want to reach the mountaintop but very few would care to climb the mountain for themselves. Do not allow the enemy to operate with smoothness in your life. *Proverbs 8:35 says, "For whoso findeth me findeth life and shall obtain favour of the Lord."*

The word of God instructs that the spirit knows the spirit by the spirit. Jesus has a powerful spirit that frightens the enemy away. His spirit is unique; it has healed the blind, caused the lame to walk, given many others a more than conquering attitude. His name (Jesus) has delivered many and entrapped the enemy under their feet. There is great

There Is Anointing Powers In Your Hands

power in the name of Jesus. *John 10:18 says, "No man taketh it from me, but I lay it down of myself. I have power to lay it down, and I have power to take it again. This commandment have I received of my father."*

Jesus had the power to lay down His own life and to pick it up again. He too has the power to pick you up and to anoint the works of your hands.

We were not created to be powerless, or to be non-achievers. We were created to be more than conquerors because we are created in the image of God. Everything is possible and you will win as long as you have *The Anointing* working inside of you. The enemy cannot control you if you do not allow Him. God wants His force behind you so that the enemy will flee. Everything that you put your hands on, God wants to bless it because He wants you to prosper. *1 John 5:4 says, "For whatsoever is born of God overcometh the world: and this is the victory that overcometh the world, even our faith."*

God wants you to look upon your hands and see Him work at large through you. If He said you could, then it shall be done. Know that JEHOVAH

There Is Anointing Powers In Your Hands

is able. *The Anointing* is in your hands, so lay your hands on it. It does not matter how big or small, wide or deep, God said just lay your hands on it. As you begin to lay your hands on it, you will see God's work in action. Remember as you move, God moves through your effort. If David would have never tried to fight Goliath, the story could not have been written; it was because of his courage to fight that the battle was won. As he fought Goliath, God gave him the power to win. It is your life, so therefore you must be willing to fight for your freedom by wanting out enough to fight your way through. Get to work. Your vision wants to live, it needs life and your hands have the power to do it.

In all that we do we need to be faithful in our doings. *I John 5:15 says, "And if we know that he hear us, whatsoever we ask, we know that we have the petitions that we desired of him."*

Our desirability needs to be strengthened by the putting on of our hands. Saul could not fight this battle because he did not have the faith he needed to win. He had never put his faith in God. However, David had enough faith that saved a whole army. Saul and the Israelites faith were filled with doubt.

There Is Anointing Powers In Your Hands

They had it set up in their minds that Goliath had already won the battle. However, David's eyes were fixed and immovable on the powers of his living God. David had no doubt in his heart; he knew he would win because he was a believer. This is an example of *no matter how many attempts to fight the battle*, without faith it will be impossible. When you reach an impossible battle, you will have to have the armies of the living God fighting in you. With just one stone, David killed Goliath. All it took was for him to pick up the stones and to place the one stone in position. In addition, as David placed the stone in his hands, God placed His strength in David. *Psalms 28:7 says, "The Lord is my strength and my shield; my heart trusted in him, and I am helped: therefore my heart rejoiceth: and with my song will I praise him."*

As David shot the sling, the force was too powerful for Goliath. It instantly killed him. David had the armies of God fighting through Him. Notice David only took one shot. His one attempt to defeat the giant was enough to measure his faith. His trust in God was so great until all he needed was a sling shot with one try. David's belief destroyed the giant before he took his first shot. Though the giant was

There Is Anointing Powers In Your Hands

standing in position before David took his first shot, in his eyesight the giant was already dead. David did not use his strength but His Father's. God used David's hands to put His strength in them. Let God *Anoint* the works of your hands. *Psalms 16:8 says, "I have set the Lord always before me: because he is at my right hand, I shall not be moved."*

Through the strength of David's hands was the strength of God residing with Him. As with David, God wants you to look at your hands as a needed tool for survival and conquering power. God's armies of power can reside in you. With your hands, all things will be blessed. Faith is movable through your working ability. Many writers have overcome their writing journey with the use of their hands. Every warrior that gained the victory has overcome using his or her hands. God wants you to put your hands on it. He will begin to stir up *The Anointing* and it will be powerful in you. When you put the Lord first in your life, God will find favor for you. David desired to please God. You must have a child-like heart's desire for the Lord. David grew up knowing the Lord as a young boy, and He longed after God's heart.

There Is Anointing Powers In Your Hands

David, had a willing heart, not a contrite heart. He did not consider the size of his hands even though man looked at him as just being a child. David never doubted that God could not use Him to fight. Think of a child in the army. He said, yes I will. David achieved through his faith in the Spirit of God. His heart inquired of his next move. He allowed himself to be a witness for Him. David exalted God wherever he went and set God's needs before his own. He had a unique love for God; David loved to let JEHOVAH know that He was God in his life. Surely, you have giants appearing in your life, step up to the plate. Let God use this battle to empower you.*Psalms 28:8 says, "The Lord is their strength, and he is the saving strength of his anointed."*

Move and walk by faith, show the world that He has all power. You may look small and be young at heart but you have a strength that is ready to work through you. It is the Anointing and nothing can defeat the Anointing, because the Anointing destroys every yoke. Get ready to defeat your giants and be prepared to come out on top. As you win this battle, everyone will know that you are a *faith walker*. What if David would have never laid his

There Is Anointing Powers In Your Hands

hands on the sling shot, be a *faith walker* and lay your hands on it.

Press and Push ... Press and Push ... Press and Push ...

The Anointing Power of your Hands

CHAPTER 3

The Heart of your Hands Beating at Work

Your last resource is always your best. The last shall be first and the first shall be the last. Just when you think things are not going to happen, God will appear. God loves to take the least of all to get the job done right. Hebrews *11:3* says, *"Through faith we understand that the worlds were framed by the word of God, so that things which are seen were not made of things which do appear."*

Many people have had the same opportunity as David but they failed. Saul looked at Goliath and feared. He had all the Israelites standing with him in fear. No one in their human mind would actually

Press and Push ... Press and Push ... Press and Push ...
stand up to this giant except David. Out of a whole army, He had the Faith that God would not let him die in this battle. Goliath was a known champion and He had never been defeated. We see things appearing before our eyes and some have caused us to fear the battle, but God wants you to move through your fearful state of mind. God does not want us to ever fear our situations, neither be afraid of going down in the valley. There is power in the valley and you will receive it as you come out of it. David realized that the times he was in the valley, he gained greater power from God. Every trial has a war time. One will be fighting against another. If you really want your vision to speak, it is time to fight for it. Now it is your time, to step forward and face your giant. Show everyone around you that you have The Armies of God fighting in you. Often times, we have to prove it to ourselves. It is time to pump up your belief and believe deeply in God that your visions are going to speak. Exercise your faith by remembering all the many challenges you have overcome with The Powers of God. This faith in God is going to cause you to say yes to His will and yes to His way. David continually reached for the heart of God. Regardless of his size, he depended on God to be his help. God gave him the desires of his heart. He has been known to many bible scholars to be listed in *the hall of faith*. Moreover, as many denounced, laughed, criticized and talked about David, God used the smallest one in the crowd with

Press and Push ... Press and Push ... Press and Push ...

no skills of basic training to defeat Goliath. Imagine Saul as all the Israelites were standing with Him; none had the courage to go against Goliath. David was not old enough, he did not stand up to their statures but David was ready to win this battle. However, in the eyesight of God, David was the perfect candidate to defeat the giant. God knew the size of David's faith. Remember, David was just the shepherd boy. He was only caught up in the midst because he was delivering food to the unit. Know that God is always in the midst. Though he was small, God fit all the power He needed in David to kill the giant. God loved the way David loved Him. He adored the way David believed in Him. David knew that God was the one that kept his heart beating through the works of his hands. *Psalms 75:1 says, "Unto thee, O God, do we give thanks, unto thee do we give thanks: for that thy name is near thy wondrous works declare."* God was the centerpiece of David's heart.

There must be a time to grow larger than self and the only way you can is to be enlarged through The Anointing Powers of God. David had a repentant heart towards God, he was very conscientious about any mistakes that he had made. He never grew too large for God to be his supremacy. He never boasted in self because God obtained the glory. Surely, David made many mistakes through his lifetime. He was human just

Press and Push ... Press and Push ... Press and Push ...
like you and I but he kept trying to please God. David did not allow his sins or any mistakes stop him from trying to please his Living Go *Psalms 51:10 says, "Create in me a clean heart, O God; and renew a right spirit within me."*

Though we have all made many mistakes we should not let them stop us from trying to please God. Do not let those things stop you from winning your battle. Beating the enemy is God's full purpose for your life. God gains more as you win the victory. Beat the enemy with the good works of your hands. The day that you begin to wash your hands from all vanity is the day that God gains greater glory. You will gain The Power of Righteousness. Everything in your life will begin to come together. God wants Excellency from us. At times, it seems as though things can never reach that manner but they can. Your hands are going to possess The Anointing Powers of God. However, they must stay prepared and ready to be used by Him at all times. Your heart is going to drive your hands to the Anointing. And once your mind is made up in Him then you will do excellence in life. *James 4:8 says, "Draw nigh to God, and he will draw nigh to you. Cleanse your hands, ye sinners; and purify your hearts, ye double minded."*

If you take the opportunity to get closer to God, then surely it will make your vision speak

Press and Push ... Press and Push ... Press and Push ...

sooner. I remember many years ago in my life, I went to church because of tradition. I never went on my own free will or because I wanted to be there. Perhaps, I went because it was Sunday or I needed a blessing. These are the two major reasons many people go to church. A vast majority only go when they need a blessing. Going to church was not a priority for me. All those years I went in the wrong state of mind. I could not tell you what the preached message was even before altar call, but I could tell you what the choir sang and how good it was. Through those years of my life, I stayed the same and I had no power. Many times, we do not develop in the manner God wants us to because we are not trying to please Him. What is your life speaking today? Do you have a David Spirit or a Saul Spirit? God wants you to impress Him. Once you impress Him, then He will cause you to give others a better impression of living life with Him. Many will be inspired and impressed by you. Your spiritual leader is the one that feeds your life. David was fed through His faith and God continuously fed him power to be victorious. Be properly fed through The Spirit of God and stay nourished. David truly knew God. *Romans 10:17 says, "So then faith cometh by hearing, and hearing by the word of God."*

    Some things that are causing conflict within your spiritual growth needs to be cut out of your life. I do not believe that many people realize the

Press and Push ... Press and Push ... Press and Push ...
many blessings that sin keeps them from. It keeps many great things away from your life. If many could see what they miss out on, they would be sick. Love your freedom and love living life itself as God created you to. Understand the word of God and experience real joy. There is so much life in the word, it will keep you empowered. Sin causes us to suffer more than one way. I have learned that it is not hard to cut sin out of your life, once you begin growing to a greater faith with God. Anything that is crippling your faith or causing you from putting your hands on the powers of God, let it or let them go. Get to know who He is. I was held captive for years, all because I did not understand His word. However, after I begin to get serious with my spiritual maturity, I grew in the word. It gave my life power. I do not mind offending sin by loving God greater. Sin has held me back long enough. I do not want to offend the God I so greatly love, need and appreciate in my life. Study the word for yourself, so that you can know the kind of God you serve. The Anointing releases you from bondage, it blesses as it covers your life and it brings forth peace. The Anointing gives you supernatural strength and it will cause you to be a winner at all times. It destroys the yokes and you will never have to carry another burden for the rest of your life. It will completely take care of you. **Is sin really worth The Anointing?** *Romans 10:17 says, "So*

Press and Push ... Press and Push ... Press and Push ... then faith cometh by hearing, and hearing by the word of God."

The Anointing Powers of God will flow through your hands. Want to stay close to Him, know that cleanliness is next to Godliness. Lay your hands on the things that God would have you to. I want my hands to be clean and pure for God so that He can operate His anointing in me. One day I received a dying emergency phone call and God told me through my prayer life that I had an anointing in my hands. He said, "For anything to work that I must lay my hands on it." Now going to this hospital for this dying emergency I needed God right then and there. Often times, people need God vessels to stay pure. Moreover, God needs us every second of the day to be prepared to be used of Him. If we are too dirty to be used our prayers may not be answered as we need them to be. This was an emergency and only The Anointing could heal this child. Imagine if I would have been living a double minded life, waddling in sin. Perhaps, The Anointing would not have been able to work through me in prayer for this child. On the other hand, what if I did not know the word of God, I would not have trusted Him myself. There is more power than you realize in the word of God.

John 1:1 says, "In the beginning was the word, and the word was with God, and the word

Press and Push ... Press and Push ... Press and Push ... was God." The word gave me a purpose and a reason to stand, just as David. In any emergency, you need The Anointing ASAP. I needed the Armies of The Living God to ride with me, walk with me and to fight for this child's healing immediately. I prayed for this precious child. This child was in intensive care not expecting to make it and the family needed God right then and there. This was a dying emergency that needed The Holy Ghost immediately. I felt the power of God flow through this prayer to heal this child. I am a firm believer in prayer power because it is the Holy Communion between God and His ordained vessels. If I was full with sin, then probably God would have not used me. However, that child needed The Anointing immediately to work powerful in healing her body. It took every day of the last six years of my life to reach this kind of Anointing with God. I refuse to allow a sinful nature to come and destroy The Anointing that God has bestowed upon my life. I refuse to let a little measly three-letter word such as sin, control any blessings that God wants to bestow in my life. In addition, I refuse to jeopardize my eternal Glory to walk on the streets of Gold and destroy my eternal life. Now you can either seek God first at everything in your life or perhaps you can keep letting The Anointing just pass you buy. **Do not allow a sin to control, guide, lead or the enemy to prepare your future.** God deserves that Glory, just give your heart to Him daily. *Mark 7:5*

Press and Push ... Press and Push ... Press and Push ... says, "Then the Pharisees and Scribes asked him, why walk not thy disciples according to the tradition of the elders, but eat bread with unwashed hands?"

One day God enlightened my heart. I just knew that I needed the word. Then I begin applying every word that I started receiving to my personal life because if one receives the word then it needs heart application. No one can grow larger in the word without it being a heart application. If you do not have self-control then the Word of God will teach you discipline. It will cause your heart to desire after righteousness. You will not be able to live in the same manner you used to. You will change for the better and you will not be the same. Your ears will not want to hear the things they use to. Your legs will not want to walk in the places they used to go. Your eyes will not look upon the things in the manner they used too. In addition, you will have a change of heart on many things in your life. Your life will have a purpose to love God as you will desire to please Him. I am a firm believer that many people go to church in such a familiar way (traditional). Nevertheless, many of people have forgotten to seek the way that God wants us to worship Him. I cannot seem to praise God as my mother did because I had to find my own praise. I cannot clap my hands like my aunt, because I had to feel the power of The Anointing clap through my hands. We cannot look on our fore fathers and the way they worshipped God, for we must find Him for ourselves. You must worship Him, as The Spirit of God will teach you how. *John 4:23 says, "God is a spirit: and they that worship him must worship him in spirit and in truth."* No matter how righteous we grow in the word, there is a need for continual washing of your hands before eating of the bread of life. You want to be pure and ready for God. Go to church with a mind prepared to receive Him. Get involved with the service and be inspired through the word. Treat the Word of God as your daily food, it will feed you new life. It will nourish your soul and lift your spirit. The Word will cause you to run when you want to quit. It will fill your heart with inspirations and keep you working on your vision. It will feed you hope in a hopeless situation. In addition, it will strengthen you where you are weak. The Word of God will bond you with The Anointing. *Romans 10:17 says, "So then faith cometh by hearing, and hearing by the word of God."*

I had to find my way to God by the putting on of my own hands. I had to open up the word of God for myself. Lay aside the things that will cause you to reject your personal faith growth. Research things on your own to grow spiritually. Many things I had to leave behind. I could not serve God as my parents did. I had to find my own way with the reaching

Press and Push ... Press and Push ... Press and Push ... forth of my praise and with my hands. I am not a firm believer in many traditional things because I never wanted to make tradition a God in my life. I believe in the God that I serve. He is so powerful, loving and caring. He will nurture your soul with righteousness. Know that He takes excellent care of your needs. God wants you to reach high for Him with the putting on of your hands. He will show you the way to The Truth and The Light. Let Him shine through you. *Ecclesiastes 9:10 says, "Whatsoever thy hand findeth to do, do it with thy might; for there is no work, nor device, nor knowledge, nor wisdom, in the grave, whither thou goest."*

The only thing that is keeping your hands from working is you. It is up to you and it will only be achieved through the measure of your faith. I am going to work my hands as long as I have the strength of God in them. Want the works of your hands to achieve in the might of God. Nothing should stop you from receiving The Anointing. That life you are dreaming about can either be a gazing dream or you can begin reaching forth with the bareness of your hands, to obtain it. Let your vision be set free. You need your hands to work towards this vision and your fingertips to grasp this moment of hope? God would not have given them to you. Just think of your index finger and everything it is willing to point out to you through the power of God. However, remember as you grab, just place it

Press and Push ... Press and Push ... Press and Push ...
within the centerfold of your hands and begin to notice God as He will work in you. Hold on to the promise that God has given you because it is all in the palm of your hands. The more you begin to use what God has given you, the more you will be able to see Him work through you. In addition, as you begin to work this particular thing just watch how God will begin to anoint the works of your hands. God wants to keep your hands clean so He can bestow greater power beyond your imagination through the work of your hands. God wants us to use our hands not of our own might but through His might. Work through His might and see that it has already been done. You must believe in the powers of God. Jesus did and He received all power in His hands. He worked His Heavenly Faith. Let your faith work for you, it will take you as high as you believe. Your faith will pull you out of every valley that you enter. It will cause you to win every battle and you will be more than a conqueror. Faith has no limits.

Understand that through your might you are inspiring hope and through hope is your power. It will increase your faith possibility. Every time you think of the works of your hands do not look at the work of your hands as impossible. Look upon the possibilities if you use them correctly. Your hands have strength that you need to exercise daily. The vision that God has embedded in your mind, use

Press and Push ... Press and Push ... Press and Push ... your hands to work it. *Habakkuk 2:3 says, "For the vision is yet for an appointed time, but at the end it shall speak, and not lie: though it tarry, wait for it: because it will surely come, it will not tarry."* The Anointing will bring you out of all that you are going through, just use your hands.

Often times, people that are striving for something strive too hard of themselves and not enough in God. Striving in self will destroy your vision but working with The Anointing will bring it to pass. Surely, God wants us to strive but not in our own might. God simply wants us to believe in Him and through Him that it is possible. God wants us to live life in abundance. For many of years I tried by my own might and I continued to fall. I realize that all the visions God had given to me were through His ability. I struggled to strive. I analyzed every possibility and I kept coming up with remarkable ideas. Nothing seemed to be working out. I had to learn patience. *James 1:3 says, "Knowing this, that the trying of your faith worketh patience."* No, we do not like to wait, especially when we want things to happen right now. However, I learned to be patient with God. As God gives us vision, He will then give us a plan. Only through His power shall the plan be developed. Remember when God gives you a vision it is greater than you. So therefore, you will need His assurance for protection of your vision. God does not intend for us to overwork

Press and Push ... Press and Push ... Press and Push ...
ourselves until we are purely exhausted. He intends for us to rely on Him. He loves being God so therefore let Him be the God over your vision. Let Him work His anointing powers through your hands. God is going to astonish you as you see it develop with your eyes. This work is going to simplify many things in your life and bring closure to your giants. *John 13:3 says, "Jesus knowing that the Father had given all things into his hands, and that he has come from God, and went to God."*

All of the works that Jesus accomplished came by The Anointing that worked through Him. Jesus sought the direction, approval, and guidance power from JEHOVAH before He made a move. Heaven was His strength as He earnestly prayed. Regardless of what accomplishment, Jesus did it all to glorify His Father. Jesus intended His Father to strengthen Him in everything leaving Him out of nothing. We too must appear to God in the same manner as Jesus, reverencing Him. He needs to be in full control over everything in your life. Your prayer is your strength and you can accomplish nothing perfectly out of this life without God's full gratitude and permission. If God is in it and if God gave you the vision then surely God is going to be your help. Jesus prayed tremendously unto His Father. He did not stop until God spoke to Him. Often times we pray but we do not give God the opportunity to speak back to us. Many say it does

Press and Push ... Press and Push ... Press and Push ...
not take all day to pray but it may take a while for God to speak back to you. I do not believe in putting a time limit on my prayer, neither do I like to rush my prayer. It is just as if you are rushing someone out the door because you have something else to do. We should not allow anything to hinder our prayer life nor to rush our communion with God. Sometimes, God takes His time to listen and then He speaks to us. Kneel down with an expectancy to finish hearing from the Lord before you prepare to get up off your knees. Just imagine if Jesus would have gotten up too early off His knees as He talked to God then He would not possess all powers today. He would not have given God the opportunity to instill heavenly power inside him. Think on how much we leave at the prayer table all because we did not take the time to listen to God and rushed as we prayed. Mark 14:38 says, Watch ye and pray, lest ye enter into temptation. The Spirit truly is ready, but the flesh is weak.

Jesus knew that His life was only because of His Father's powers and so therefore, He never had to analyze, think about or wonder when and if He needed to pray. Everyone in this world needs The Power of Prayer to make it through. Just as you and I, Jesus had to overcome many things. He suffered tremendously. People went against Him and He too had a mission. It was to save you and me. All because of your vision, many will be encouraged.

Press and Push ... Press and Push ... Press and Push ...
You need The Power of prayer to get you through. Jesus was very attentive unto His Father through prayer. Jesus needed Heavenly Powers to conquer the world and God gave them to Him. He will also give you the power to conquer. Every work was because His Father led him first, guided Him through and gave Him the power to achieve. He listened to Heaven as He prayed. Many have asked the question, "How do you know when God is speaking to you". Truly it cannot be explained, for every one hears Him in a different manner. However, you will know His voice. Once you believe that your prayers have reached heaven, then He will speak clearly to you. You will hear Him as you will begin to follow Him. As you kneel, be prepared to hear what God has to say to you. *John 10:27 says, "My sheep hear my voice, and I know them, and they follow me:"* Your prayer life is of your own free will. The power that God will bestow in your life is up to how much power you are going to need in a lifetime. Jesus made sure He received all the power He would ever need. He continuously knelt down in prayer and God continuously gave Him power.

I needed the strength of God to help me stand against the wiles of the devil. I also needed the strength of God to help me continue in ministry. I could not walk as a minister in my own power for I needed heavenly powers to help me. My power is

Press and Push ... Press and Push ... Press and Push ...
nothing if God is not the author of it. I cannot defeat the enemy without the Spirit of God. The enemy will choke you down if you do not have heavenly power. *Hebrew 12:2 says, "Looking unto Jesus the author and finisher of our faith; who for the joy that was set before him endured the cross, despising the shame, and is set down at the right hand of the throne of God."* He wants your hands to be strengthened with prayer power for the work to be completed. God wants you to seek His face and pay great attention to Him for He speaks power into your soul. As you prepare for your new prayer life be prepared to receive greater powers from heavenly places. They will inspire your spiritual growth, as well as others that are around you. God is ready to give you heavenly powers that you never knew. Be prepared to do the wondrous works by the putting on of your hands with the anointing power of God. He is a God of action and as you begin your new prayer life, God is going to act on your prayers. Just remember to never stop praying for it quenches your spiritual growth. Continue to pray every day as though you are praying for the last time. From this day forward, you will become more powerful. Know that God moves as we pray and He listens as we speak to Him. Heaven will hear you, as it will open the doors of blessings to cover your life. Jesus knew the many secrets of God and He received His powers. Get to know the secrets of God and be empowered.

The Anointing Power of your Hands

CHAPTER 4

Spiritual Inflammation

Your prayer life is about to be appealingly altered to a spiritual inner sense. God reveals His secrets to the righteous. It will unite a flame within your heart that will cause a reaction for God to move within your life. As you pray, God wants you to feel the flame of His power moving all in you. I consider it to be Spiritual Inflammation. God wants to move as a flame of fire in your prayer life that will burn any hindrance of your spiritual growth. Your prayers are going to reach God in a manner that He will consume the forces of the enemy out of your life. It will be as a piece of paper, that has fallen into a fireplace and it is at its highest blaze. The more you pray, the more God will begin to exalt power in your life. He will give you revelation. *Psalms 88:10 says, "Lord God of my salvation, I have cried day and night before thee:"*

Press and Push ... Press and Push ... Press and Push ...

    David continually cried out to God because he needed to constantly be strengthened. Though David fought many battles, he needed God's strength at all times. It is all right to cry out and let God know that He is your strength, you could not survive without Him. David wrote many Psalms as he earnestly prayed. He simply always longed after the mercies of God. He needed to continue to endure his many life challenges. When you need to endure, just pray. God will give you what you need. David wanted freedom and every time he called out to God, He freed David. *Colossians 4:2 says, "Continue in prayer, and watch in the same with thanksgiving;"*

    Often, we look upon ourselves as being all-powerful, because we do not take the time to kneel down in prayer. Prayer is an open relationship between you and God, because as you speak He listens and as He speaks then you can hear. In order to achieve a greater accomplishment you need the Anointing. A sure way to receive the Anointing is to have a communicable two-way relationship with God. Speak to Him and He will speak back to you. However, you need to watch as you pray so that you can hear Him. *Luke 21:36 says, "Watch ye therefore, and pray always, that ye may be accounted worthy to escape all these things that shall come to pass and to stand before the son of men."* How can you hear Him if you do not take the time to listen in prayer? Be considerate of God's needs as you pray. Always expect a response from God in prayer. You must pound on Heaven's doors like it is an emergency. Prayer will open up the floodgates of Heaven when you are praying in the Spirit of God. If you would take the time to exercise your prayer life, then God will build you with His anointing. The Anointing will cause you to have powers from heavenly places. As we grow, we must become wiser. Are you tired of unanswered prayers? Pray until God changes everything in your life. I learned not to settle for less especially when I realized that God has all power to give me the best. God never created us to settle, prove your belief in Him by showing Him your faith. Expand the level of belief and expect to live a greater life. Though it may take you a little longer to get what you want, remember He saves the best for last. Ask what you want and He will answer you. Sometimes, I do not ask God because He will just simply give it to me before I ask. Believe that you are special to Him and He will treat you special. Seek God in prayer until you get His attention and He will inflame His spirit in your life. *Ecclesiastes 4:5 says, "The fool foldeth his hands together, and eateth his own flesh."*

In the beginning of my prayer life, I never understood why I loved to pray at night. Often times, I found myself kneeling in the midnight hour.

Press and Push ... Press and Push ... Press and Push ...
Even sometimes, as I was sleeping, I would wake up out of a dream and begin kneeling in prayer. Oh, prayer is the most traumatizing time of your spiritual growth. Prayer will develop a special bond between you and Him and you will grow powerfully as prayer begins to inhabit your life. I say that because many things will begin to happen. I often thought I was losing my mind when I begin to hear voices speak to me. Sometimes, as I was praying I also begin to see little white lights. I did not know what was going on. Then, there were times I was in church when I began seeing things and I would often know things before they happened. Prayer will introduce you to the Spirit of God. It does not matter how you feel, if your body is tired, aching, or even if you are deep in sleep. Many times, I did not feel like praying but something powerful moved me to pray. It was unexplainable what came over me. It was that particular prayer, on that night that drove me into The Anointing. Perhaps, it was because I just needed to catch up with my prayer life. Often times, many people pray but not in The Spirit. Sometimes, you do not realize how selfish your prayer life can be. People think prayer is only for when you want to ask God for a favor or you have a need. God just wants us to communicate with Him; He wants to talk to you. Just as you desire true and honest relationships in your life, then so does He. In addition, just as you want someone to listen to you, God wants the exact same thing. *John 10:27 says,*

Press and Push ... Press and Push ... Press and Push ...
"My sheep hear my voice and I know them, and they follow me." As the Spirit of the Lord speaks, His children will know Him. Too many times God is ignored by people that just do not want to listen; it's simply because they know it all or just do not want to follow. Well, one thing I know, God is not going to make anyone want to hear Him. Anyone that desires to be heard by Him will eventually follow God. *Psalms 88:2 says, "Let my prayer come before thee: incline thine ear unto my cry;"* David wanted God to hear him, so he prayed and He prayed. He too had experienced many troubled times, but He could not let his troubles over take him. David trusted God enough to listen to him. When you begin to pray more spiritually to God then spiritual change will intercede with an utterance from on high. Things will begin to change and you will receive power. God will listen, if you take the time to speak; he will answer. God wants you to give your troubles to Him. God will save you in your time of your need, just depend on Him. He does not expect us to do things on our own. However, He does expect us to need Him at all times. Prayer invites the Spirit of God to be your life protector; He would love to be a part of you. Though many ran away from God because they were too busy noticing their faults, David still ran to Him. David knew there was only one to deliver Him and it was God. He did not mind calling on God, after all God had carried Him through so many

Press and Push ... Press and Push ... Press and Push ...
troubling times. David figured if God brought me through that then surely He could get me through this. *John 5:25 says, "Verily, verily, I say unto you, The hour is coming, and now is, when the dead shall hear the voice of the Son of God: and they that hear shall live."* God will speak to you but first He just wants to hear what you have to say. It is just like meeting someone that you really do not know, instead of you doing all the talking you really just want to listen. I have noticed that if you listen to what someone has to say in the first conversation you will get to know them pretty well. In talking to God, He is able to show you just who you are. He will guide you to the full assurance of His anointing power. Now, many different things are going to be rearranged and fully altered in your life. God has a way of moving things around in order to get us right. JEHOVAH is a God of change and He loves to decorate our lives. His specialty is to decorate our lives to become beautiful. He is going to make your life peaceful. However, some changes must ultimately take place in your life. These changes will have to occur in order for your life to be fulfilled. Once God begins to work on you, be prepared for a complete life makeover. *Psalms 88:3 says, "For my soul is full of troubles: and my life draweth nigh unto the grave."* David simply needed God's help to pull him out of a world of troubles. Many times many people cannot accomplish their goals because of their lack of knowledge in the

Press and Push ... Press and Push ... Press and Push ...

Powers of God. Only a fool will fold his hands on his vision but the hands of a wise man will make it. God will give you the strength to follow through with your vision. However, if your faith is not in Him, it will not work. Keep your faith in God, not in yourself. Many men have let themselves down; do not be one of them! The hands of a man that will allow critiquing moments without getting offended will cause him or her to become great. Know that it is only God who has given you a vision. Stop allowing the pressures of being a failure to interrupt your vision. The vision that you have must go forth. The truth shall speak through the works of your hands. When you really put your mind on the things that God has allowed so many to accomplish, why should it be too hard for you? God knows and many others see it in you. If God did not think that your hands could bare this particular work, then He would not have given it to you. The vision would not have ever surfaced. *11 Corinthians 3:18 says, "But we all, with open face beholding as in a glass the glory of the Lord, are changed into the same image from glory to glory, even as by the Spirit of the Lord."* Yes, God already knows everything He needs to know about you. Nevertheless, do you know exactly who He is? In the beginning of your prayer journey believe me, your life is going to be completely rearranged. Moreover, you really do not know who you are until God introduces you unto yourself. Get ready because God is going to put a

Press and Push ... Press and Push ... Press and Push ...
new definition to your name and He is going to define you through your prayer life. You will begin to be able to speak with His authority and possess His powers. God is ready to spiritually develop you. You must go deep to know the true depths of the powers of prayer. You will never pray live or be the same. There is so much power in prayer but you have to go deep in order to receive it. In the name of Jesus, I claim you will receive The Anointing. It is time to speak to God like never before and He will speak in your life. Men will be in awe at the power of God in your life. *Matthew 4:17 says, "From that time Jesus began to preach, and to say, Repent: for the kingdom of God is at hand."* Most parents tell their children to pray but many never teach them how to reverence the Lord in prayer. We all are raised with some form of biblical stories, personal testimonies and family experiences. The question becomes, what have our elders, parents and family members really taught us about the Spirit of God? Now that is deep. Yes, they spoke of God but did they explain to us that we must get to know Him in a Spiritual manner. After all God is a spirit. Surely, we have seen somebody pray, and yes, we know how to bow our heads, as well as folding our hands while we pray. Did anybody really take the time to teach you to pray in the Spirit to God? Did they tell you to pray until you feel the Spirit of God move on you and to pray until God says that He is satisfied? That only comes after you feel the Anointing move

Press and Push ... Press and Push ... Press and Push ...
all over you. Did anybody tell you how the power of prayer really works and why you need to pray? Most of us just heard, remember to say your prayers before you eat, say your prayers before you go to bed and pray when you wake up. Others wrapped it up and said, "Pray three times a day." I tell many when you kneel down to pray regardless of how long it takes, just pray until you feel the Spirit of God move all over you from the inside out. Prayer is not something that needs to be rushed. It is the most delicate part of your spiritual growth. To be a true life achiever you will need The Anointing. Prayer will ultimately improve your life. *John 4:23 says, "But the hour cometh, and now is, when the true worshipers shall worship the Father in spirit and in truth: for the Father seeketh such to worship him."*

God has been waiting on you all of your life, just to notice that He is God alone. God loves attention, He loves His authority and He wants to be glorified. God wants a personal and true relationship with you that no man can ever depart or interrupt. He wants to answer your prayers, just so you can believe that He is God. He simply wants to talk to you. God loves it when we acknowledge Him. He loves receiving glory. He wants you to inherit a life that will be richly blessed. I often tell people that God just loves to show off His working powers in us. Through your prayer life, God is going to restore many things that you have lost. He is going to work

Press and Push ... Press and Push ... Press and Push ...
everything out just as He has always done in your life. Try praying to God, as you know Him to be your life restorer. Release your heart to God, it will be the best thing that you have ever done. *Psalms 89:17 says, "For thou art the glory of their strength: and in thy favor our horn shall be exalted."*

Prayer is one of the holiest communions that anyone could ever have with God. He loves the ones that reach towards His heart through desiring Him. God loves us to kneel down in prayer to Him, it is just like visiting someone and they are glad to see you. Have you ever been in a relationship and enjoyed that particular person but really with all honesty never loved them. It is like if they are there, who cares and if they are not, who cares. But when you grow lonely you think about them and it's all for selfish personal gain and then afterward you do not care again. I know it might sound harsh but the truth is the truth. In prayer, most of us are too busy speaking and we often do not give God the time to say a word. God wants us to feel His presence, and become closer to Him. We all need improvement in the spiritual development (prayer). Be ready, excited and wanting to feel His Spiritual touch. Every time you kneel to God, you are reverencing His worth. Care about how you make Him feel. *Psalms 68:19 says, "Blessed be the Lord, who loadeth us with benefits, even the God of our*

Press and Push ... Press and Push ... Press and Push ...
salvation. Selah." God waits on us daily in preparing that His faithful will come forth. He blesses us more than we truly deserve. God loves full respect and He loves to be glorified. **He blesses us every single day of our lives that we still have blood flowing through our veins.** Every time we open our eyes and see throughout the day, we are blessed. God touches our limbs to be strengthened enough to move every day and that is worth a moment of true worship. Daily we are fed for nutritional purposes and daily we are sheltered, that is another reason to truly worship Him. For many years the enemy did not steal my joy. I gave it to him every time I did not kneel down in prayer; every time I did not take a moment to worship. God is waiting on you every day to just worship Him. He does not intend you to wait until you get to church to worship Him, He wants you to worship daily. So therefore, when you get to church you will know the truth. You will be able to join in with your praises as you worship Him in Spirit and Truth. Our prayer life covers us daily. I owe my life to Jesus because He laid down His life for me. So therefore, I am in debt to Him. I take nothing for granted because I appreciate the God that I serve. No weapon that is formed against me shall prosper because my Father, which is in Heaven covers me. Know that He is your covering. God is waiting on you to worship Him in Spirit and in Truth. A true prayer life opens up the truth of spiritual communication between you

Press and Push ... Press and Push ... Press and Push ...
and God. You will begin to form a spiritual worship just between you and God. The performance of *The Anointing* is getting ready to work mightily in your life. He wants to anoint the work of your hands. God wants to bless everything your hands will ever touch. In addition, He is going to make it all happen just for you. *Psalms 88:15 says, "I am afflicted and ready to die from my youth up: while I suffer thy terrors I am distracted."* We all have been guilty of kneeling just for a need and then as soon as that need is supplied we find ourselves forgetting to kneel in prayer. Many times, we have allowed things and people to distract our prayer life. They have caused our spiritual development many distractions. It is time to draw closer to Him and farther from the distractions. We do not really think about prayer until something happens and then we need God again to work it out. Often times, many people receive an immediate blessing but sometimes many do not get what they prayed for. I learned that throughout the years if we would not stop praying, then we would not have to keep starting over and over again. When you take the time to get to know God Spiritually the truth will unfold before your eyes. Prayer will build your confidence in Him. That is how simple our prayer life should be with God. Ignoring the presence of the Lord will cause great hindrances in your life. It's just as you call out to someone and they do not answer you. God does not like to be ignored. His presence is full of the

Press and Push ... Press and Push ... Press and Push ...
anointing and that is the point where you want your prayer life to be. *James 5:16 says, "Confess your faults one to another, and pray one for another, that ye may be healed. The effectual fervent prayer of a righteous man availeth much."*

Showing God consideration will greatly enrich your life to become more powerful. It will invite peace to come into your life. Confession opens the blind eyes and your faith will be your sight. When one confesses, it will make the truth appear because their faults will no longer be hidden. Often times, many people will not acknowledge their wrongs, but once one confesses, they will. Confess with your heart and God will come in and perform miracle after miracle, just for you. He will show you things and He will teach you His secrets. God will make all things right in your life. Your vision will gain more power, as your hands will gain Supernatural Strength. The troubles in your life will begin to cease. Your faith will increase in Him and His powers will flow smoother in your life. No matter what comes your way, talk to God about it. He listens and as He does, He moves. Prayer will simply cause Spiritual Inflammation to increase in your life. The Anointing will flame righteously through the works of your hands. The prayers of the righteous will always avail, and surely, your vision will speak boldly.

Press and Push ... Press and Push ... Press and Push ...

The Anointing Power of your Hands

CHAPTER 5

Praying to the Point of no Return

    Children depend on their parents to take care of them. That is how God expects us to depend on Him. God wants us to be prepared for Him to take care of our needs. He is a jealous God and He does not want us to put anything before Him, not even our love ones. God wants us to glorify Him first; He also wants us to appreciate Him daily. For many years He has tended to the care of our families by ensuring us to wake up in the right state of mind. He has given us the ability to care for them. God wants our attention in Him. Could you imagine your child not paying you any attention for days, weeks, months or years? They see you every day, and live with you while you have bent over backwards looking after them? God wants you to also care

Press and Push ... Press and Push ... Press and Push ...
about Him. After all, you would not have made it this far without God. *Matthew 6:6 says, "But thou, when thou prayest, enter into thy closet, and when thou hast shut the door, pray to thy Father which is in secret; and thy Father which seeth in secret shall reward thee openly."*

Prayer can only surface through your heart and God knows our hearts? That is why He needs to be positioned first in our life. When you come to God with a true heart, everything will be set free in your life and there will be no more secrets. Your life will be purposed to satisfy Him. God deserves better from us. He has a better plan for our life that is why He gives us vision. He wants us to see that we could have a better life, just kneel down in truth. Let God inspire you like never before. For the first time in your life, feel pure and know that your change has begun. It will be like no other prayer in your life, God delivered me and He will do the same for you. When He moves you with The Anointing every unjust thing will be served an eviction notice without warning. Immediately, He put claims over your life and the enemy will flee from your heart. You will never forget that prayer, because that prayer caused your soul to be delivered from hell. From that day forward, you will have a new start. *Psalms 105:15 Says, "Touch not mine anointed, and do my prophets no harm."* God will touch you and put His Spirit of Calmness to live in you. If

Press and Push ... Press and Push ... Press and Push ...

things in your life are troubled hold on to His word. You have immeasurable powers in the inside of you that are not yet speaking for your life. God is a God of full reward, He evens remembers the way we bless Him in secret. He only gives us our heart's desires. God gives us the liberty to make our own choices. Nothing can stop or hold God back from working powerfully in your life but you. Satan does not have the power over your future if God is in control of your life. All you have to do is kneel down in prayer with an expectancy to be delivered. Just kneel with an open heart, and watch God fulfill you. Though some things may later try you, God will not let it touch you. His covering will speak to the enemy, touch not my Anointed.

Bow when you are in need, speak to God with your heart and tell Him you desire to love Him. He will teach you how to love Him; satisfy Him and He will satisfy you. *Psalms 90:14 says, "O Satisfy us early with thy mercy; that we may rejoice and be glad all our days."* Listen to God as He will speak to you and allow Him to lead you into His presence. God loves you and He will satisfy all your heart's desires. God said, He will give us our heart's desires and when we begin to desire Him every need will be given to us, and every prayer will be answered. Just imagined how powerful that day will be not just for your life but also for everyone that is exposed to you. That is Anointing Power. God will make you

Press and Push ... Press and Push ... Press and Push ...

glad. He will change your life in a manner that you will begin to rejoice every day in Him, just because. 1 Thessalonians 5:17, *"Pray without ceasing."*

As you begin to pray, there is no need to stop. Notice every time you stop the enemy forces himself into your life. Through the years I too have begun praying and somewhere along the way I stopped. I had to start all over again from square one. Developing a prayer life takes time and it is not going to happen in the blink of an eye. Prayer develops through our prayer experiences. It takes time to build towards a never failing faith. God's timing is different from ours and His pace is at a supernatural flow. If God stops being God for a day, tell me how He can supply us mercy in the time of our need. Look around at the hospitals, millions are on life support daily throughout the world. They are living not by life support but by prayer support abroad through co-workers, church members, friends, family and even sometimes the prayers of strangers. Many will join their forces together to pray in such a needed time and God is going to answer someone's prayer. You never know whose prayers God is answering first. I do not know many people that will pleasantly open up their front door to a stranger, even after the fact that they have properly introduced themselves. Well, that is how God is to us daily. He opens up His windows of Heaven to look out and see just whom it is calling

Press and Push ... Press and Push ... Press and Push ...
upon His name. In addition, if it is an unfamiliar voice then there is much proof you will need in order for God to open up. Just as myself, it has taken me years to receive my prayer power. Just as David stayed in touch with God we too must keep our relationship with God. I have endured many hours of tears, prayers, church settings, worship hours, Holy Communions and study-time in the word, just to reach this point in my life. I have worked hard for God to get to know who I am. You must continually prepare by folding your hands in prayer and never stop the Spirit of God from moving in your life. I cannot count the prayers day and night that I lifted up or the tears that rolled down my cheeks. No matter what comes your way just continue to pray. Yes, many things are going to try you, but keep on praying. The enemy works for a purpose to keep us away from God. Do not give into any more excuses and do not let him keep you away from God. *Psalms 91:1 "He that dwelleth in the secret place of the most High shall abide under the shadow of the Almighty."*

Jesus gave me the opportunity to the tree of life and I am forever grateful unto God for that opportunity. See, if you really ever noticed the tree of life, there are branches and connected to every branch there's hope, love, faith, guidance, rewards, heavenly things, favor, power from on high, due inheritance, Anointing, life eternal, blessings,

Press and Push ... Press and Push ... Press and Push ...
assurance, increase, prosperity, good things, healing, miracles, and everything that is dead is ultimately brought to life. To make it easier for you to understand, daily you and I have the opportunity to receive all these and so much more. An opportunity is not something that is forced on you, it is something that only you can realize the true value of and appreciate its worth by accepting it with great gratitude within your heart. His presence will shadow your ground and cover you always. *1 Thessalonians 5:19 says, "Quench not the spirit."*

Every time you have stopped praying, you have allowed the enemy to come and rearrange your life. Know that you need The Anointing. You must continue to pray without stopping. Nevertheless, when you stop praying it puts a halt on the anointing to flow in your life. You have an opportunity to receive the powers of God by folding your hands in prayer. We all have the opportunity to fold our hands in prayer and to gain power from on high. In most cases, many give the enemy power over their prayer life by not praying. Let God shadow your life. Satan knows when we are not covered. A faithless prayer life intoxicates the blessed life that God wants for you. When people walk in such stumbling conditions, it is an embarrassment and it's not showing that God lives in you. However, it does show the world that you are off balance, unstable and you are walking without the power of

Press and Push ... Press and Push ... Press and Push ...
God in your life. God wants to shadow your life so get covering in prayer. *Psalms 91:4 says, "He shall cover thee with his feathers, and under his wings shalt thou trust: his truth shall be thy shield and buckler."*

Every second within an hour someone needs God's attention that is how busy He really is. Can you imagine every emergency that is going on at one time throughout the whole world? That is how busy God really is, He does not have the time to sleep, rest nor slumber. He is a very attentive and watchful God. He is always taking care of His children's needs by being a God with deep concern. Do not leave home without prayer. Treat your prayer life as if it is your insurance policy, make sure you are covered. Troubles are always waiting to occur and you do not want to encounter trouble without being fully covered. David was one that was covered by God; he was under the shadow of The Wings of God. He took the time to get to know God. That is why he was always covered. When he fell, He was covered, as he stumbled David was covered and as he battled, God covered Him. Make sure you are covered through your day as you leave home and before you lay to rest at night. However, the more you pray, your insurance policy increases with Him. The more you pray it upgrades your trust in Him. Satisfy God with your prayer. *1 Thessalonians*

Press and Push ... Press and Push ... Press and Push ...
5:18 "In everything give thanks: for this is the will of God in Christ Jesus concerning you."

One thing you must begin to understand is that God loves you. Jesus suffered too much for you to take this opportunity of life for granted. Never take your prayer life for granted and never let the enemy scare you. Jesus' whole life as He walked the face of this earth was to prove His love first to His Father; secondly to you and thirdly to the enemy. Every work that He did, He uplifted, exalted and glorified His Father. Jesus is the prime example that you can overcome, you can conquer the enemy with power but you must stay prayed up. Jesus intended us to pray as He did. He took the time to teach us to pray. All along, He was showing us how to honor His Heavenly Father. Jesus separated himself from many to pray and He was teaching us how to follow Him. Jesus took His prayer life seriously because He was guiding us to His Heavenly Father. He is the guide to Heaven. You need guidance; if you do not take the time to pray then you will never receive it. God has a perfect plan, specifically for you to live and God wants your lifestyle also to be promoted. He wants others to see how He will bless those that are obedient to His words. There are so many people that are watching and waiting on you to make it, they are noticing how God is working miracles out for you. Our life speaks for itself but is it truly speaking that God lives. God wants you to

Press and Push ... Press and Push ... Press and Push ...
obtain a supernatural lifestyle that is going to cause many more people to kneel down in prayer. You must pray, because your power to overcome is in the way you kneel down and reverence God in prayer. Things may appear not to be going in the manner you would have wanted them, still be thankful. God wants us to appreciate everything in life including the bad. God is in full control of our lives and sometimes He does not always allow things to go the way we want them because of the plan that has just for your life. Through the years I've learned to thank God for everything, it's a wonderful thing even during your hard times that you can still thank God from the depths of your heart. *Matthew 6:7 says, "But when you pray, use not vain repetitions, as the heathen do: for they think that they shall be heard for their much speaking."*

Just imagine if you are given a certain task to do but then when you leave you never consider your instruction and the importance of them, how are you going to complete your task sufficiently? Surely, you want good things to happen in your life but are you prepared to do what is needed in order for you to achieve? There is a time in your life for everything and now is the time for a real serious prayer life. As you begin to care about your prayer life and the seriousness it has over your life then God will begin to take good care of your prayers.

Press and Push ... Press and Push ... Press and Push ...
Once you become deeply concerned with the cares of God then God gets concerned about blessing your prayer life. So therefore, at no time can God afford His time to be wasted. God's time is so valuable because when you are not praying, believe me, there is someone else receiving His full attention. God wants you to pray in the truth, not being concerned about big revolving words but merely just opening up your heart to Him. God does not need another person to pray aloud just so others can hear; God needs a prayer warrior that is ready and willing to fulfill His desires. Many preachers love to pray openly on the roster but many of them even pray without power. What good is it to pray one day out of the week just because people are going to hear you and then you have not knelt down on your knees to pray all week long? God knows us through our secret closet, He knows every time we truly pray unto Him with sincerity from our hearts.

Growing Prayer Power

In order for anything to grow it takes time. If you want real prayer power then you need to give it time. First, if you do not sow the seed of prayer then how can you expect to gain the power in your prayer? Regardless of whatever it is that you want to grow in your life, growing is a process it simply just takes time. Over a certain period, God will enrich

Press and Push ... Press and Push ... Press and Push ...
your prayer power. I often say that if you want something done then you must do it yourself. If you really want God to hear you then you need to begin speaking to God for yourself, kneeling down continuously in prayer. I have learned over the years that sometimes we can exhaust ourselves in prayer and it is due to insufficient prayer power. Because how can you pray without power. It takes power to surge anything, it takes the power of electricity to turn on the lights. Surely, you can flick the switch on but if the power is disconnected then the lights still won't turn on. If you put the key in the ignition and turn the key switch in your car but the battery is dead then how is it that the car is going to start? Then if you are out of gas and you try to turn on the diesel generator, then how is it that your power will come on? Without everything being properly prepared and connected for correct operation, one powerless thing will stop all the other power from surging. *II Corinthians 5:7 says, (For we walk by faith, not by sight :...)*

God wants you to be motivated not through your sight but by your faith, encouraged not through your sight but by your faith. And He wants you to be fully prepared at all available times to be able to receive just what He has for you. He wants you to keep your mind stayed on the finished work not the beginning of the work or even care about the trying times of the work He has given you. He doesn't

Press and Push ... Press and Push ... Press and Push ...

want you to focus in on your own ability, your own strength nor your own capabilities but on His powers that He wants to surge through your prayer life. The work of your hands is needed to either return to working your vision or begin planning your dream to unfold to life. For many years I too prayed but I prayed powerless. A powerless prayer will exhaust your prayer life due to the fact that it's hard praying and still no change. If you really want your life to change, then your prayer must change from powerless to become full of the anointing. In addition, God has all the anointing power you will ever need, just put your hands on it. Get thirsty in your soul for the anointing to overtake you. In order to start anything and especially an anointed prayer life you need power from on high. A certain essence gets the power surging in your prayer life. God yearns for a true prayer warrior and Jesus was one of the best. I can imagine that He summed it all up in the model prayer of teaching us how to pray. Still I fully believe that He knew; He had faith that God had already taken care of His needs so therefore the majority of His prayers were for other people's needs. Jesus never had a selfish heart when He prayed. Therefore, as you pray your heart must be clear to God and a selfish heart will never reach God's own heart. *James 5:16 "Confess your faults one to another, and pray one for another, and that ye may be healed. The effectual fervent prayer availeth much."* You never know when you are

Press and Push ... Press and Push ... Press and Push ...
going to need a dying emergency from God. It is so valuable to stay prayed up with His Anointing because it's truly up to you how much you are willing to value your prayer life with God. There is no sense of praying and you have no power. In order to receive power from God you must first crank it up. How can a car start without the key in the ignition and baby you cannot hot-wire a prayer. The key to cranking up your prayer life is to kneel down in the correct way to God. As you begin to kneel, you must be prepared to kneel down with an open heart, readily to confess your wrongs. See, in every case the addict will not confess their faults in the beginning until the addiction has overtaken them. For so long the enemy has entrapped our minds, hearts, bodies and souls because we are not honest enough to confess our own faults, because more than often most people are too busy pin pointing other people faults. Wrong is wrong and right is right. It's just like walking into a situation blind folded but if so many would have knelt down to pray before they begin their day then so many would not have experienced that demon addiction, doing something crazy, getting arrested, raping someone and the list can go on. See, you never know what the end of your day will bring that will forever change your life. Many wish they just had another opportunity to go back in time to change what they have done wrong but you just can't turn back the clock. That is why it is so valuable to pray

Press and Push ... Press and Push ... Press and Push ...
even before you begin your day. I believe no one intended to do wrong but many are just caught up in their wrongs and one wrong thing just leads to another. No, God does not want you to dread on your past but He wants you to do what is right now, He wants you to get a new mind set and that is to keep your mind on Him first. *Matthew 26:41 says, "Watch and pray, that ye enter not into temptation: the spirit is willing, but the flesh is weak."* That is why it is so valuable for us not to stop praying because we must tune in to the Spirit of God first thing in the morning as we begin to open up our eyes, whether it's day or night that you wake up, it's time to pray. Do you ever think to pray to God to lead you not into temptation? Just imagine, what if 50% of every human being that is truly guilty of their crimes are sitting in prison or on death row had prayed this prayer alone? Every wrong temptation that is upon the face of this earth is a tempting spirit of the enemy to attack our spiritual development of happiness, good health, wealth and prosperity. God is a God of assurance, love, deliverance, freedom, hope, peace and joy. All of these equal the goods that will develop out of your spiritual life through the power of prayer. As you begin to watch you will then begin to notice that, nothing can go forward in your life without the power of God authorizing it and allowing it. See, many of us get to a certain point where we just can't bare life as it is and we realize that we want more. But in wanting more you

Press and Push ... Press and Push ... Press and Push ...
can only get it through God so now you are prepared to expect a difference in order to receive what you are seeking out of this life. Prayer is so wonderful because it is so powerful. Prayer is the key to opening up God's heart to flow into your life. I begin praying like never before in the year of 1999 and as I prayed this particular night, I did not give it any thought. I just knelt down but as I begin to kneel down, I knew that before I knelt, God was going to hear my supplication. I went to God like never before, feeling a deep urgency and I needed immediate attention. The way my heart felt this night was like no other night I had yet experienced, I longed for God in a manner of confessing my wrongs and all I wanted was for God to make me right. I went down expressing everything from the inside out. I begin pouring out my heart and even until this day, I cannot tell you exactly how long. When I knelt down it was nightfall but when I rose up the birds were singing and the sun had risen. Within this night of prayer it was the most beautiful night I ever had, I felt poor and needy going down but I rose up with power. I do not remember everything but I know that God was all in it. I believe he answered every single need for the rest of my life just through this one prayer because God felt my heart. I did not kneel down in doubt but I knelt down in true fear for my life, soul and family - I knelt down in faith. I knew what I was but I also knew that only God could change me. This prayer

was my life changing prayer; God wants to change your life from being powerless to becoming all powerful. He wants to anoint the work of your hands and He even wants to give you the greater works. *James 5:15 says, "And the prayer of faith shall save the sick, and the Lord shall raise them up; and if he have committed sins, they shall be forgiven him."* You must begin something new that you never had in your prayer life in order to get God's attention immediately. See, the Spirit of God is so willing to change your life and as long as there is a will of God surely there is a way. You must not trust yourself (flesh), because you are weak and you will fall, if God is not in it. Even Jesus had to kneel and He is powerful but He never stopped kneeling to receive His power. Everything Jesus did was because He wanted His Father's heart to be happy. You must have the same spirit of willingness to pray so that God can will you His Spirit in the time of your need. Jesus never looked through fleshly eyesight because He was always seeing through His spiritual eyes. Jesus allowed the Spirit of God to feed Him His Spirit daily. Think of it as your vehicle that you drive around the city and your gas begin to run out and sooner than later, you will need to fill up again. I always think of my prayer life that way because it's a hurting feeling when you run out of gas and I don't ever want to run out of power from on high. You never know what situation you might encounter that you will need the power of

Press and Push ... Press and Push ... Press and Push ... your prayer to get you or someone else out immediately. I pray earnestly because as God fills me and as I go on I need more of Him. As you continue your new prayer life, the enemy is going to try to grow larger and stronger in your life because He wants to stop you from praying, but you just remember that God is larger than all the enemies put together. The enemy loves to try to throw you off balance and to catch you off your guard. One thing you must understand is that the more spiritually you grow the more powerful you'll get and if you have the power of God completely on your side then the enemy can't touch you because of your Most High All-Powerful God that is guarding your life. The enemy cannot over power God and that is why God needs to be in full control of your life and not you. *Luke 11:20 says "When a strong man armed keepeth his palace, his goods are in peace."*

As you continue to pray with power and your prayer power is increased with spiritual essence from on high, your covering begins to shield your area. Many leaders have asked me during the time of our ministry growth, do you have a covering? Throughout these years, there were so many Bishops and leaders that wanted to cover our ministry but the spirit of God always said to me, "I am your covering." Building a ministry is harder than you could ever imagine because you pray, sow, and work yourself to the bone for people just trying

Press and Push ... Press and Push ... Press and Push ...
to get their attention span to stay focused on the word of God so that God could change their lives. In addition, the harder you work in the ministry it seems as though the less they will do. All these years with people confessing what God has told them to do for the church and they still do not do it. I sometimes used to get so angry because I got tired of hearing so many fables and tales. However, as I continued through an almost seemingly impossible fight I realized that I started fighting for a more fervent prayer life. I got so tired of their excuses, and they continued to provide one. One of the favorite ones is that I have to work, for so long I told people the reason you are working two jobs is that you need strength from the Lord. I have never seen the righteous forsaken, forgotten nor left behind. Living life for self will cause forces from the enemy to seclude your mind, praise, prayer life, worship, gathering of the saints and even get you to a certain understanding that what you are doing is right. I consider it an addiction of confusion, walking blind without power because they know not how to pray. If God has blessed your life and if you keep on your Armor of His Spirit, you will never have to worry about the enemy tearing down your house.

    I will never forget a sermon my husband preached, "How bad do you want it?" Man, did I grasp it. Being a Christian is one thing, but it's a completely different aspect being a powerful

Press and Push ... Press and Push ... Press and Push ... weapon of a Christian holding down your palace. There was a time when our oldest son needed to move in with us, I believe he thought I was crazy. There were certain things that I just would not allow to go on in our household. If it were not of God then I could not allow it in. Even though He just wanted to listen to regular music, I said, "no." The enemy travels by many different ways but if we stand our guard, as we ought to then He cannot overtake our homes. And on Sundays everyone must find a place to worship. If I am at church praising God, praying, singing, worshiping then I mean for everyone to do the same in my household. There is a time in our lives that we must not take any form of power for granted. If I am praying then I must train my whole household to pray with me as well as for me. In my house we are going to serve the Lord. God wants you to stay protected through His spirit and keep daily watch over the things that we allow in our homes. A True Believer that is of great power for God must stand their own ground even when they can't see it they still must stand just because of their faith. You cannot allow any and everything in the world to be in your homes. I am very prayerful in my home, over my home and even after someone leaves my home. I believe in the power of prayer and it is stronger to me than I know my first and last name.

    I had to come to realize in my life that absolutely nothing will separate me from the love of

Press and Push ... Press and Push ... Press and Push ...
God; no excuse is allowing to come out of my mouth. No reason is good enough to give to God and no one is greater to me than He is; therefore, I love expressing my devotion to Him. I believe that when you begin to really care about your prayer life then you will begin to care about God. Just as many people have asked my husband and me, "Do you have a covering?" Come on, these are Pastors and leaders who are supposed to be God fearing church leaders. God is our covering because Jesus showed me and led me to my Father. I have had more church people to go against us than worldly people but I did not let that or they stop me from praying. I looked upon their belief and the way they treated me and I prayed more earnestly not to be another one of them. See as our church was growing in the year of 2004/2005 God blessed us with a building that many thought was a disgrace because of the unfinished, broke down and terrible look of the building. We needed a roof, flooring, walls, electrical work and so much more. At this time, we only had about 17 old members and about 8 new comers (adults not including their children). We had quite a few additional fellowship church services and you had better believe more people looked down on us instead of lending us a helping hand. We prayed and sent letters to all the churches in the city of Charlotte and to most of those big television ministries and only five churches responded with help. In addition, two individual people blessed us

Press and Push ... Press and Push ... Press and Push ...
without asking from the heart to try to help us. However, all the leaders that wanted to cover us never lifted one finger to help us unless we signed over our ministry to them.

No we didn't have to take that church in its condition but I prayed and asked God for an area that needed us and if that is the building that God blessed us with then I was thankful and so were some of the congregation. We must understand how precious our gratitude is to God because He said that if we can be faithful over a few then He would add all things unto us. In that broken state of a building was God's fortifying plan for our ministry growth, development and our heart's began growing more spiritually. Within these bare walls and leaking roof, God supplied us generous mercy because we appreciated what He had blessed us with. The power of prayer was able to surge greater power within our lives through the Fountain that begin replenishing our lives with power. For within this messed up building through many man-made eyesight's was the beautiful presence of the Lord. He woke up something in the inside of me that I thought I already had. He gave me a heart to yearn for the righteousness in others that was walking on the outside of this building. See, there were many prostitutes, drug addicts, children fallen to the wayside and this community was a laughing joke to many. God blessed my heart to feel their need to

Press and Push ... Press and Push ... Press and Push ...

want their change so that many others can see their beauty through the power of God. I knew this job was greater than my husband and I put together. My husband, who is our Honorable Bishop, I love so dearly for believing in the power of God that he never gave up on our ministry, neither did He give up on me. This job needed the anointing of God to overflow and spread abroad. So then I had to begin a deeper prayer journey. No matter how good you begin to pray you will always need to take a deeper plunge in the Spirit of God in your prayer life. The passion that God has given me to help others was great and mighty. *John 17:9 says, "I pray for them: I pray not for the world, but for them which thou hast given me; for they are thine."*

See, while many walked out of this ministry because of our workload, the needed amount of finances to operate this huge mission and the unity that had to be enforced, they missed something that money just could not buy. Instead of you putting your eyes on the amount of creativity of your mission; the hardship that it is going to take to make this all possible, just remember that God moves in every impossible situation. No matter what our circumstance was, I believed God for the greater. I never looked at our needs and thought that God could not do it. I realized here in this mess of a building that God needed to gain something from me that before I just did not have. Many of our

Press and Push ... Press and Push ... Press and Push ...
members missed out on their faith inheritance and spiritual development because God never wanted us to feel the pressure of getting this building done. He wanted us to see how so many souls have been undone spiritually. For this opportunity was one of the deeper faith unities that God had ever embarked on the Fountain of Life Christian Ministries and my personal life. Sometimes, God will try your heart just to see where you stand. Even though He already knows you, He just wants to show you something that is going to add greatness through His Spirit to strengthen you with pure powerful faith. As you look on the things within your life that seems impossible, I am here to tell you that it is all possible. I do not care how bad it is, just remember, "How bad you want it." If God gave it to you then it is already yours, stop letting the things of this world get you down but allow the powers of God to lift you up. Put your hands on whatever it is that God said for you to do and never focus on the impossibilities of your vision, but keep your mind focused on how God can make it all possible just for you. *Luke 14:18 says, "And they all with one consent began to make excuse." The first said unto him, I have bought a piece of ground, and I must needs go and see it: I pray thee have excused me.*

Luke 14:19 says, "And another said, I have married a wife, and therefore I cannot come." I grew through all their excuses, the members that

Press and Push ... Press and Push ... Press and Push ...

quit, the churches that did not help, the love ones you thought you could depend on, and the people that did not support. Because every obstacle that came our way, God just picked it up and moved it and we were able to make it again. I thank God for everything He has done in our life but I knew that it all was done through the power of prayer because God answered us every time just in time. God is our covering but we must ask Him, can He be the God in our life? For with the power of God as your armor you will gain power far beyond your imagination through your prayer life, until the enemy will tremble as you speak. As I continued growing spiritually in this process, I knew that it was all God and not I. I knew that God listened and answered our prayers. Nevertheless, I could not stop praying, I felt the yoke of Jesus around my neck plenty of times. I wanted to quit sometimes but the power of God would push me down on my knees and bring me back to remembrance of what He had already done within our lives. I know without a shadow of a doubt that God is our covering and that no other man on this earth could cover us like God can. God is the only keeper of the Fountain and of my life. The only time most men help you is when they can get something out of it and I refuse to give them that glory for my God deserves all the Glory thereof, because He's been by my side when I couldn't depend on anyone else not even myself.

Press and Push ... Press and Push ... Press and Push ...

Often times I just break out in praise because I know, and when you know something nobody can change your mind. I thank God for His Son all the time because Jesus has truly been my role model. When you realize the power that your prayers hold, peace will begin to surround everything within your life. Regardless of how bad things will sometimes get, you must not focus on the bad things in your situations but you have to focus on your victory through the power of prayer. God does not want to hear our excuses or bickering complaints, He just wants you to believe that He is, He will and know within your heart that He is God. Never put anything before God, He is waiting on you to open up your heat so that He can expand His Anointing Powers to the work of your hands.

The Anointing Power of your Hands

CHAPTER 6

Seven Keys to Prayer

Key One: Respecting Jehovah

Imagine if you had all the right set of keys to open every door you needed in your life. I mean never having to wish, want or crave for anything but just having pure power to gain it all by reverencing your Heavenly Father because you know He is fully at work in your life. *Matthew 6:9 says, "After this manner therefore pray ye: Our Father which art in heaven, Hallowed be thy name."*
Jesus knew that God would always take care of His personal needs, as well as his spiritual needs because God was within Him. Jesus worshiped His Father from His inner soul and adored Heaven from the depths of His heart. His worship in prayer was a fervent private worship that kept Him connected to

Faith Without Works Are Dead. Press and PUSH ...

His Heavenly Powers. When you open your prayers with respect and honor, and as you worship, this brings God's Spirit into you. God's Spirit will move deep in you. His Spirit will begin to caress your soul as you worship Him. Truth will arrive in your mind, as He will show you the way. As you commune with God, He will begin to change you from the inside out. Heaven will open as it fills you with His presence. Now, realizing how hollowed your Father in heaven is through your worship effort from the depths of your heart, God will begin to conduct your life and He will declare things to flee from you. Notice the scripture, it possesses the first key to providing you with the method of receiving Anointing Powers from Heavenly Places. Jesus knew the manner to pray which is the method for our Heavenly Father to be our life conductor. Surely, you know a conductor's duty is simply just to make things perfect. So therefore, take notice towards this manner because without True Worship we just simply cannot enter into the presence of the Lord.

John 4:22 says, "Ye worship ye know not what: we know what we worship: for salvation is of the Jews." For many of years, many have gotten it wrong as they pray. Though they believe that they are seeking God, truly they are seeking for material possessions. Many are worshiping God in the wrong manner, which simplifies the wrong method of prayer. God knows our needs and He has provided greatly for many of us but often times we worship our blessings, possessions, and things. We consider them to be miracles. God wants you to worship Him because He is The Great I Am. His name is Jehovah, which is The Most High. He is Jehovah Nissi, your banner of hope, life forevermore. God wants you to worship Him because He has freed you from bondage, and He has taken the keys of Hell through His only begotten son.

John 4:23 says, "But the hour cometh, and now is, when the true worshippers shall worship the Father in spirit and in truth: for the Father seeketh such to worship him." Once you know Him in that manner, no one will have to remind you of worship because your heart will be driven with a love passion to worship Him openly, freely, truthfully and spiritually. Worship covers your life with His daily blessings. God is 100% Pure Spirit, His presence will cause you to walk in agreement with Him. God wants you to recognize who He is, respect, honor and Exalt Him to the fullest. Worship ushers you into The Presence of Righteousness and God begins to justify your life. True worship releases The Anointing to destroy the yokes and to tear down all strongholds. It unleashes Heavenly Power to surround your atmosphere and to walk before you. Now as you enter into His presence through your worship, you will also enter into His

Faith Without Works Are Dead. Press and PUSH ...
Kingdom powers. Every time you worship Him in The Spirit, God justifies your life. Just as the woman with the issue of blood, her way of worship was in her press. She had her eyes fixed on her determination to touch the presence of Jesus. She no longer felt her pain, claimed her issues, it was His virtue that drew her near, until she touched The Anointing. Once you begin to worship, you cannot feel anything but God moving in your life. Nothing at this point will stop you from moving into His presence. Your mind is not your own, your being is filled with freedom and your atmosphere is now in His presence. However, troubles that caused issues to ruin your life will ultimately disappear, no tears of sorrow but only joy as praise will utter out of your mouth. You are now at the point of no return, old things are passed away and now the newest has been effectively promised to you. God has ushered you into His presence, where no weapon formed against you will be able to prosper. You are now at the point of no return. The many things that periodically caused issues to come in your life will not trouble you any longer; no storm will wipe you away. You are now at the point of no return. This is the most valuable key that will cause your prayers to be ultimately heard by Him. You will have supernatural prayer power.

Key Two: Matthew 6:10 says, Thy Kingdom come. Thy will be done in earth, as it is in heaven.

Faith Without Works Are Dead. Press and PUSH ...

    We acknowledge there will be a day for God's Kingdom to come again; we know that the Day of Judgment is a day that will come; therefore, you want to be ready. God reigns in His Spirit daily in heaven and heaven is impossible without the presence of God. Daily, that same Spirit of God can reign in your life. When God reigns He reigns anointing powers, complete healing, full deliverance, sufficient grace, perfect mercy, happiness, beautiful joy, abundant blessings, pure faith, greater love, magnificent meekness, caring gentleness, perfect peace, inspiring hope and so much more. The things that God reigns are not man-made but spiritually granted unto those that are true to God in prayer. Daily, God's will is performed in Heaven with the works of His Heavenly Powers and today God can provide you that same power while you are on this earth. It is vital that you believe in the heavenly powers because all of His children's help comes from heavenly places. You will have no worries once you know that God is in full control. Often people tend to worry but when you are in God's will, there is no worry. I always pray Father let your will be done in my life because through every will there is a sure inheritance. Daily I want God to will to me my inheritance, what about you? The only way to be put in a will is that someone must feel your needs. They must want something greater for you to have, because they have seen that

Faith Without Works Are Dead. Press and PUSH ...

you deserve it. I do not know anyone that will just will anything to anybody without knowing him or her personally or without seeing someone's effort at work. As you seek God in prayer, you too will notice that everything He has allowed in your life was perfectly fit for a great purpose. In addition, everything that He will begin to do in your life is perfectly designed just for you. Allow God's will to be done in your life, for he knows what is truly best for us. God knows your needs, He knows your wants and He will give you your heart's desires. God is a perfect God and He is the Father of perfection. So, allow His will to be done in your life because He will bring you heavenly things that the enemy will have no control over.

Key Three: Matthew 6:11 says, Give us this day our daily bread.

You want God to feed you what you need to be properly nourished for life. Daily, you need a word to support the true factor of God and not only needing that daily feeding just for nutritional purposes but more for spiritual development. Within the word of God, there is life more abundantly, power in the word that will incorporate your life to be abundantly satisfied and life from the enemy. You want God to give you exactly what He knows that you need. Many of times we go and supply our own needs and never realize until it is too late that

God did not intend us to have it. God is a perfect provider; He is not going to give you more than you are prepared to handle. God supplies our needs in perfect proportions. Daily, I want God to provide me with what He wants to provide me with. In the *NKJ version* it states that man cannot live by bread and water alone but by every word that proceedeth out of the mouth of God *(Matt 4:4)*. I want God to feed me daily as I hunger for more of Him because His word is true and daily His word sets me free from the enemy. As you pray, you will want freedom because in freedom you are able to put your hands on things that will add greater things in your life. There is a certain spiritual feeding that you are going to need just to get to your next level. It takes time to grow spiritually but it is up to you to want to earnestly invest into your prayer life spiritually. The only way to receive The Spirit is to go into The Spirit. Go after God, seek Him daily, pray to Him earnestly and allow Him the opportunity to grow in your life. Let Him be magnified in you and through you as you endeavor to go deeper into your spiritual prayer life.

Key Four: Matthew 6:12 says, "And forgive us our debts, as we forgive our debtors."

Regardless of our daily efforts, trying to be the best believer we can, we all tend to make mistakes, knowingly and sometimes not knowing at

Faith Without Works Are Dead. Press and PUSH ...

all. Daily as you pray kneel in forgiveness. When you seek for God to forgive you then you need to have the same loving compassion in your heart to forgive others. I have seen family members that are serious church people and cannot even forgive their own brother. Still, we expect God to forgive us daily of our sins but then we harden our hearts to people that need our forgiveness and love. I have done so many wrong things in my lifetime that I asked God for forgiveness and He forgave me. When we seek forgiveness of one it clears the heart and conscious of the wrongs. Forgiveness is one of the most important factors of seeking after the presence of God because it cleanses the heart of impurities that the enemy has power over. God is a forever forgiving God and therefore we need to have the heart of God to forgive others. Never hold a grudge because many are doing time every day on death row in prison, or even have already passed in this lifetime all because of an unforgiving heart. I would not personally want to be one trying to appear to God in seeking forgiveness and cannot forgive my own brother or sisters. Just as God has no respect of a person neither should we. Just as Jesus laid down His life for us, God expects the same daily out of His children. Moreover, just as we ask for forgiveness of God then we need to learn how to forgive others daily.

Faith Without Works Are Dead. Press and PUSH ...

Key Five, Six & Seven: Matthew 6:13 says, "And lead us not into temptation, but deliver us from evil: For thine is the Kingdom, and the power, and the glory, for ever. Amen."

God knows us and He knows everything about us big or small. Just as God knows how we are because He sees our inner secrets, He knows of everyone's temptation, because we all are born in the flesh. Some form of flesh is going to try to rise up; however, neither you nor I have the power to control it but God does. You never know what is ahead of your day until it is over regardless of what's on your agenda. The enemy knows all of our weaknesses and that is how he tempts us so much. The enemy controls temptation and he is the author of deceit, destruction and killing. Daily Jesus prayed too because He had to, acknowledging that temptation was all around Him. So therefore, Jesus did not want to be lead into temptation and we must pray daily in the same manner; this is Jesus' method of receiving power to overcome all that is against you. Now, if Jesus walked the face of this earth with great power and authority, then we must do the same. Do you realize that if many people would have knelt down to pray for God not to lead them into temptation then they would have a second chance at life? You never know what you are going to encounter throughout a day. Therefore, prayer must be first on your list of things to do. I never

Faith Without Works Are Dead. Press and PUSH ...

leave home without prayer because it is never a guarantee that I will return home. Moreover, if you notice, temptation is everywhere you go. It is on your job, around the corner and it lives as we live daily. As long as you continue to go throughout this life without praying to the Father, you will not experience your Divine Purpose in life.

Many people, such as prisoners, people that have contracted terminal diseases, drug addicts, prostitutes, liars, cheaters, stealers, robbers, murderers, molesters, adulterers, falling pastors and the list goes on, could have had a better life if they had taken the time to pray in these seven key areas. It is so valuable to learn the power of prayer because the power that is in a fervent prayer warrior will get God's attention. It will release the fullness of God to be evident in your life because then the Kingdom will have come upon you. Prayer is the one key to everything you will ever need and it is the greatest weapon of defense to make the enemy flee out of your life. Prayer with power is your key to a successful spiritual life, living in the anointing of God.

As you endeavor to seek power through your prayer life, the enemy will try to tempt you in every way and try to stop you from entering The Kingdom of God. The enemy does not want you in the presence of God because then He cannot be in your life; that is why you have to take your prayer into worship through The Spirit. For many years I thought the enemy was so powerful with his evil forces but the more I grew in the power of God, the more I realized that God is more powerful than the enemy. It's just like when you were a child and that bully always aggravated you, always upset and hurt you; therefore, one day you got tired of the bully and told your daddy or mother and they rushed to your aid. When that bully saw your daddy that bully got scared, ran way and never bothered you again. I believe that He [God] sits high and looks low and He will beat up any enemy that tries to mess with me. God will do the same for you. Just stay prayerful and continue growing in the power of prayer. Fold your hands, kneel down and watch how God changes your life. No matter what comes your way, just keep praying in your faith, the more you pray the more power you will receive from God. Even in praying sometimes, you will fall but just keep praying. I have felt strong in prayer power and sometimes I felt weak in prayer power but I never stopped praying. We cannot understand everything as we walk this earth but whatever we need to understand God will explain it to us in the spirit.

Prayer life is serious and I devote my heart to God in prayer. I do not know all that He is going to require out of you, just be attentive as He begins to speak to you. I love praying because I love to hear

Faith Without Works Are Dead. Press and PUSH ...

God speak to me, He always encourages me when I need to be encouraged the most. He will give you inspiration in your weakest times and will strengthen you with the courage to continue your vision. Things have occurred in your life that sometimes tried to alter the way you would serve God, even through the closest ones that you love but thank God for being your true comforter. Depend on Him to lead your life because for many years you have done or allowed some things to mess it up. Do not run from God any more, just fix it all in your mind from this day forward that you are going to run to Him. So now through many life experiences I hope you have learned to seek God's approval first and then let Him be your guide. He has done a miraculous job in your life so far because things could be worst but instead of your many wrongs, God has still blessed you. That work that you must achieve, He said, "Yes you can," now all you have to do is to put your hands on it. Just because some things may have brought a halt to your work does not mean that it cannot move forward now. It is time for you to leave all excuses, hurts, laziness and doubts in the past because it's your moving forward time now. God wants your work in progress so that He can receive the glory for it.

The Anointing Power of your Hands

CHAPTER 7

Getting to Know Your Hands' Personality

Blessings will simply cause GOD to bless you

Psalms 50: 15 says, "And call upon me in the day of trouble: I will deliver thee, and thou shalt glorify me."

I know many times God has given you some form of creativity and as you look over your life, you may see the life changing affect it could do for you. Other times in our lives, God wants us to get ahead, instead of barely making it. If God is God over this whole world and owns everything in it then I realize that I am a shareowner too, just as Abraham. Therefore, I knew I needed to make a change in the manner that I truly praised God. I had

Faith Without Works Are Dead. Press and PUSH ...

to believe more in the talents God had given me but it could not have been possible until I begin putting my hands back to work on it after praising God for this beautiful gift. God gives us gifts and if we use our gifts to glorify Him then He will begin to glorify us. God intended us to use what we have instead of depending on things that are not yet in our reach. As I begin writing in the year 2000, I realized that I was nobody to many and who would want my writings? So for many years I continued to work in my field as a hairstylist, a shop owner and barely making it. I allowed my family to be hindered from divine prosperity, vacations; even a better lifestyle due to my insecurities and writing ability that God had given me. However, one day I realized just as Paul and Silas to never quit believing no matter what came their way. Alternatively, I begin to believe in a lifestyle that, quite naturally, my income could not supply so I begin writing more and more. God wants us to be great achievers in the word and more than anything God loves to be glorified. No matter the state or condition that many think you are in, that is how God wants it. It does not matter how many look down at you, God adores you. It does not matter how impossible things seem to be, God still wants you to use what you have and to begin until it is finished. Everyone that has been living a lowly existence and have need for a better more wholesome life, you are just perfect and ripe for God to use. If you look like you are not serving God

Faith Without Works Are Dead. Press and PUSH ...
like many others are and you do not have great possessions, then you are the perfect vessel for God to exalt. Too many, as a preacher and writer, I simply looked like a joke but God will have the last laugh. I love allowing God the praise because He is worthy to spiritually incorporate your life from nothing until it overflows with everything.

    I stopped looking at what I did not have and started praising God for all that He has given me. I knew deep in my heart that God gave me this writing ability and all those beautiful songs and spiritual books was going to set many people free one day. As long as God can receive the glory then you had better believe He is going to make a way for you. Surely, God has given you something and at one time or another you have begun to perform the work with the putting on of your hands and then you stopped because you thought you needed something else. God does not expect for us to prepare ourselves with things that can quickly fade away, but God wants us to keep it all spiritual that will cause us to yearn for more so He can continue to fill us up again as we run out of the things we need. He is a supplier of the needy, His warehouse of blessings is full and the blessings are ready to be delivered to you, but God is just waiting on your work to be complete. Just as the story of the ten virgins, five were prepared and five were not. The five that were prepared continued to be in a spiritual

Faith Without Works Are Dead. Press and PUSH ...
developing process. They did all that they needed to do because they followed through with their instructions being fully prepared and ready. Then the five that missed their opportunity was due to slothfulness because they stopped caring about their needs.

God will begin to bring forth the things as we need them for the ones that are prepared and ready. I had a great vision, but no true hope. I allowed book writings, studies, and beautiful spiritual songs to sit in file cabinets for many years. Do you think that if you had started what you had in those file cabinets; then finished that you might not be in the predicament that you are in now. If God intended it to have already happened, then surely, it would have. On the other hand, perhaps if you had kept your hands on the vision that God had given you then you would already be there. Enough with the excuses. God has given you a great gift. Perhaps, many different gifts but only one of them is designed to bring your life into glorious perfection. We can come up with more than a thousand excuses but not one of them is going to truly matter. What matters now is that you stop looking at it all to be impossible to happen in your life. God loves impossibilities and He loves us to look upon Him for our help. Whenever you are in trouble all you have to do is call upon Him and He will be there. He is only a phone call away. There is no further need to analyze your personal situation. We no longer need to waste any more precious time. Just as I was born to write, well now is my time for God to allow it to come out. There was much spiritual growing that I needed in order to mature in His greater works. I no longer wanted to be just a writer but I longed for the desire to encourage many hearts to run towards their vision like never before. Just remember if God gave it to you then you can accomplish it, I do not believe that God gives wasted or lifeless gifts, appreciate what God has given you.

Romans 12:12 says, "Rejoicing in hope; patience in tribulation; continuing instant in prayer." There will be times that will occur that something might traumatize your prayer life. When you are traumatized and something happened without notice. It was not in your plan and it was unexpected. You may either go into deeper prayer or you can get in a state of shock. In some cases, people have found Jesus in a wounded situation because it caused them to do something for God that just was not expected of them in a normal situation. In addition, in some shocking life changes some of us only know that we cannot do it but God can and He will. I feel that is how Paul & Silas felt when they were thrown into prison just because they were believers in Christ and carried the words of the Lord in their hearts. In this unexpected imprisonment,

Faith Without Works Are Dead. Press and PUSH ...
they had not the time to complain, bicker or feel their weakness. They knew this was a time for rejoicing and praying. In many of our life experiences, we analyze why, how and when. I tell many who forget because it has already by passed them that now is the time to pray. Your situation happened and needs to be over. You can never erase your past because it has already occurred but you can start the effectual change with your present, for now is the time to pray to change your future. God loves to show up in a hopeless situation because He is our hope in producing favor because our hope is God's specialty.

I know you may be thinking, "Yea right" how are your hands going to show forth a personality? How can my hands speak for me? Well, in every way of your life, if you notice a bomb you never think of how it got into that position, you only notice that their lives seemed to be bombed out. Generally speaking, most of the homeless, neighborhood drunks and so on are classified as appearing to be bombed out. How many times have you passed by one particular person that was living a low estate of life and you were greatly inspired by their achievements or even wanted to be like them? I am not talking against them because the majority of them realistically were not prepared for their fallen situations. Perhaps, they were alone and did not have the correct association

Faith Without Works Are Dead. Press and PUSH ...

to keep them inspired during their falling times. The main thing I want you to understand is that you never know what is going to happen in your tomorrow. That is why it is so valuable to fully prepare your future with the word today and let it speak through the works of your hands. We drive by and pass plenty that are beggars and the first thought that comes to our mind is that they should get a job; if I can work then so can they. Look upon one successful individual, such as Donald Trump, many would love to have his riches but so many would not and could not put forth the work effort that he has in order to achieve what he has. A man that is known of great wealth and prosperity over flowing with riches is automatically presumed to be a hard worker with a known record of accomplishment of action and effort. Your hand personality exhibits the true character that you are, it forms your character of classification, and it speaks for you even when you say nothing. Success and achievement is a photograph of who you have been in your past. No one realistically thinks about where you are going once you reach the top; they only know that now you are an achiever. Your hand does have a personality, it represents your worth to many and it is proof of your working ability. Because many people are noticed for their life's work and it is the work of our hands that motivate others. Money may answer many things but it is gone as soon as you spend it if you are not properly invested. However, a polite personality with powerful vision will speak forever and ever. Because of their great achievements and good deeds, for they will speak some form of victory, life-changing message that proves this particular individual was or is a great successor. That is the message that we all want to send to the ones that can see us, live around us and that are depending on us daily. Surely, Donald Trump did not accumulate such form of great wealth by doing nothing but he has gained greatly in his life by doing whatever it took to make it necessary for him to achieve. *John 13:3 says, "Jesus knowing that the Father had given all things into his hands, and that he was come from God, and went to God."*

Look upon the movement ability that are in your hands and think upon the life changing ability that is right there at your fingertips, after all it is your life, your vision and your prosperity. Jesus never looked on His own ability but always towards His Father's ability. He lifted His hands in the manner that God had lifted them, He believed not in Himself but He kept His full belief in God. First, understand it is the work of your hands that make you the person that you are. Your hands are distinctive; they bring character towards your personality. If you realize the manner that others perceive you, it is only because the way your hands have proven their working ability through the bringing out of your personality. Jesus proved to the world that God was in Him. God formed Him and that God is powerful. Just as you and I have a hand personality for our works so do many others that have become mightily successful with the victory. An individual that is truly tired of their situations, issues and strongholds are going to do something life changing about it. Jesus saw the workload that God had put before Him in the form of an illustration. The work was so mighty, so huge, until He knew that He needed the strength of God to do it in Him. One that is known for an achiever outcome is most definitely going to strive for greater because they are going to change their hand personality. If you are tired of struggles in your life then you will begin to do something about it by working greater. On the other hand, perhaps you will be ready to begin a new adventure such as your own business, now you are ready to work it. You will think with a new mindset being set on the Anointing. In addition, you will move with the works of your hands through the powers of God. Just as Jesus healed many by the laying on of His hands, He prayed for many by the folding of His hands and He Anointed many by the touch of His hands. You will allow the Spirit of God to begin a magnificent work through the laying on of your hands, put your hands on it. *Psalms 119:66 says, "Teach me good judgment and knowledge: for I have believed thy commandments."*

Faith Without Works Are Dead. Press and PUSH ...

One day I got tired of being just another hairstylist, standing on my feet with long rugged hours and terrible back pains and still bills galore. Certainly, I needed income but if I had never made a mind change in my life I would still be missing out on my children's tender years, being over exhausted on special occasions such as holidays and then coming home burnt out not wanting to be bothered. Right then and there I had to make a change. I no longer wanted to be a hair stylist but I wanted God to show many that everything that seemed to be impossible in their life can be made manifest. I wanted to write, sing, and minister in any way to be effective for God. I was born to lead, I was born to triumph and for many years I was what everyone else wanted but never being whom God birthed me to be. Surely, if you notice the labor, effort and works that your hands have committed to do then you will begin to realize you are what your hands have proven to be. I realized that I wanted to live in the presence of the Lord, the fullness of the Lord and no longer wanted to be what I wanted to be but to be who God could make me to be. God wants you to realize the fullness effect, the change effect and the powerful affect He can have on and in your life. He has the power right now to change, create and to make you a completely new life, but it is up to how bad you want it. He took His time to create so much in this world and He wants you to realize that if He has the power to create a whole world in a manner of days then most surely He also has the power to make your visions come to reality. That is why He has given you the vision in the first place so that you can desire it and then He will prosper you along with it. *Psalms 24:1 says, "The EARTH is the Lord's, and the fullness thereof; the world, and they that dwell therein."*

I do understand just how you feel especially when you feel all odds are formed against you. It is hard jumping through the loop holes especially when you are tired of disappointments. Whenever you are trying to accomplish something greater than you then you must prepare yourself for victory and always look towards the power of God to seat you higher. Remember, you are not doing this alone; God has full control over it, so there is no need to worry. Once you are able to overcome then you know without a shadow of a doubt that you are a born achiever. You may appear too many to be a complete failure at everything you do, well I am here to tell you that you are a perfect candidate to receive power from on high. God loves those that seem to be complete failures because they are the perfect ones for Him to receive full glory; He exalts them because they are normally a show off for God, meaning that God will receive greater glory. God cannot fill something that is already full but He has the power to fill up the emptiness. He is a God that produces fullness to the effect of running over. For

Faith Without Works Are Dead. Press and PUSH ...

the ones that believe that He is and that dwells with Him, never run on empty. Just as you may purchase something that is beautiful, you love the compliments that it is beautiful. Well, God is the same way, He can take someone who no one notices and make many people notice that He did it all and lifted them high until many will be amazed. Most people are caught off track and they cannot see achievement because of their own failures. Many have always quoted that if you are not a threat to the enemy then He is not going to bother you. The enemy does not want the children of God to succeed because when you succeed with victory you will shock many and cause other failures to obtain victory from on high. Blessed will be your first name and highly favored by God will be your last name, as the enemy will denounce himself out of your life. If the enemy can continue to throw obstacles in your pathway then he believes he will shut down your vision; then the enemy can ruin your future if you give in to him. That is why he is trying so hard to get you to quit and give up on your dreams. Whatever you do, do not listen to the enemy but follow the Anointing Powers until you reach your goal. Understand there is a reason for everything. Take this opportunity to learn from it but do not allow it to make you break. I have failed in many things in my life until I have honestly lost count but it took every failing thing in order for me to run for greater. It took every failing situation in

Faith Without Works Are Dead. Press and PUSH ...

my life to make me not to want to fail anymore. Moreover, it took me to fall that many times to depend greater on the power of God to pick me up; I got tired of getting back up so I continued to stand on the word until it lifted me. I am not speaking on the times you fall down on purpose but the mere accidents and incidents that will cause a powerful move if you are serious. It will cause you to redirect your path, it will show you the wrong from the right and it will cause God to have to do something awesome in your life.

Proverbs 3:16 says, "The length of days are in her right hand; and in her left hand are riches and honor." Think upon the days of Adam and Eve, she took her hand to eat there of the forbidden fruit, that caused her hands to fall into sin. Regardless of which hand it was, it was one or the other, definitely both of your hands have a purpose to serve in the vision that you have. When one begins the work then the other receives the reward from it. Just as Eve took upon the forbidden fruit, it caused her and Adam to come into a Sinful Nature. You must be careful what you allow your hands to touch, because for everything that they touch there will be a just reward. A hand that fails will have to just work harder towards its goals in order to achieve them but understanding the reason why they had fallen in the first place. God wants you to see the glory of the work of your hands when it is finished. What a day of recompense it shall be for you, a day in which God will be glorified through your good deeds. Notice the achievements and desired effects of the rewards but put your hands to work so that He can be manifested in it. Often times we fell but in our failures God just wants our eyes to be opened with a broader aspect of what He expects from us. As Eve took part and initiated the eating of the forbidden fruit with Adam, together they caused a chain reaction of sinful nature. God never created us to have to work so hard. He created us to be awesomely blessed but because of the disobedience, some of us are still born in a cursed generation. Well today, that curse of sinful nature can be broken. This curse can only be broken through the manner in which you allow your hands to work towards your achievements. It is almost as if you are born into a rich family, then 95% of the time you will stay rich. On the other hand, if you are born into a family of poverty, then 75% of the time you will live your full life struggling. That is the true value of being born to be blessed and just because you have already been, birth does not mean that you missed the opportunity of being blessed. If you set in your mind today on the true purpose that God created you and no longer considering your fore fathers then today God can birth you a whole new life. Every time one fails, it is only because of a minute problem somewhere and all it needs is correcting. A determined person that falls will always get back up. They will not accept their failure as a failure just a hurt and guess what, time after time your hurt will disappear. Just think if Eve, in her present state, had surrounded herself with the ability to think, would she have eaten from the forbidden fruit. Stop analyzing and thinking of your down falls. Once you realize that you were in the wrong or perhaps your hands have touched things that God had forbidden you to touch, just ask Him for forgiveness and move on with your life. Just as He sent Adam and Eve forth, God wants to do the same with you. *Genesis 3:22 says, "And the Lord God said, Behold, the man is become as one of us, to know good and evil: and now, lest he put forth his hand, and take also of the tree of life, and eat, and live for ever."*

One thing you must understand is that God is not at all like man, God is a forgiving God that gives instruction for life. Adam had to step forward as well as Eve because if they had stayed there they probably would have gone against God again. Note this, you must put forth the work of your hands; it will be a source of the ground tilling from the work of your hands. Yes, though you may have had it easier if you would have done what you were supposed to but guess what, you did not. There is a strength that is combined in the work of your hands but your eyes must see it until your hands become proof of it. You must feel this work with your heart,

Faith Without Works Are Dead. Press and PUSH...
a compassion that nothing will ever interfere with it. Now that you understand the only way it will speak is when you put your hands on it and it is finished. Surely tilling your ground is going to be hard work but it needs your true dedication with a tremendous amount of strength. I have learned through life that two hands are better than one. God wants the work of your hands to live to form your life's purpose, He wants it to be brought unto reality. *Psalms 37:24 says, "Though he fall, he shall not be utterly cast down: for the Lord upholdeth him with his hand."*

I know there are many times when I have felt that I just was not ever going to make it through. I have always felt the spirit of Job every time I felt that I was tormented without a cause. I too once was a Job traveling through much travail but deserving far greater than what I had. Not only was I true to God but also I had to encounter my patient period of development. Before I had a one on one personal suffering experience with the spirit of Job, going through waiting patiently for my God to deliver me, I just wanted to quit. Just as Job suffered greatly, I often just wondered why I was suffering. I had previously always had things in my life to go according to the way I had planned. I did not want to adjust to patience, because being patient took too long. It was an agonizing, long and a drawn out period of disappointments. Even though I prayed, it made me question myself. What was the use of

Faith Without Works Are Dead. Press and PUSH ...

continuing and trying? I know how you feel. You feel as though things are not going to ever go right in your life. You feel just as Job and I felt - what's the use of trying when everything you try just continues to fall in your face. In addition, every time failure came, it hurt because you knew deep in your heart that it all was going to finally pull together. Well, do not let the trying struggles stop you just because you have continued to try and life's failures have continued to overwhelm you. Keep trying no matter how hard things get, regardless of how impossible it seems, because "It Ain't What It Looks Like." Once my Bishop, L.D. Parker, preached a beautiful message just as I was going through my Job experience, "It Ain't What It Looks Like." It moved me greatly; from that day on, I continued to quote that exact same phrase every time I thought that all else had failed in my life, "It Ain't What It Looks Like." No matter what came my way that was trying to tear my hope down I just continued to say, "IT AIN"T WHAT IT LOOKS LIKE." As the next door slammed me in my face, as the next prayer I prayed was not being answered, and as the next faith walk I took brought forth no evidence, I thought I was not going to make it. That message carried me from 2001 until now and it will carry me for the rest of my life. I learned from that one message to look at things not like they appear; look at them as I want them to appear. I know what my eyes see but I believe not in my sight, but in the

Faith Without Works Are Dead. Press and PUSH ...

faith I have in the power of God. *John 14:1 says, "Let not your heart be troubled: ye believe in God, believe also in me."*

I can imagine that Job experience was still nothing compared to what many of us go through in a lifetime that he had to encounter just for a season. You may have bowed down, falling on your face and searching for the healing powers of God to come and deliver you out of your tormenting situation and still you feel that God is not hearing you. Surely, we all go through hard times and sometimes those trials seem to have no end, despite of all your good efforts, still no end. Well Job experienced not only heartaches but also he experienced losing everything that he had accumulated in his lifetime. Just as you have worked so hard to obtain and still it all seems to be quickly fading away almost in the blink of an eye. Surely, it hurts and most definitely it is a hardship that is over loading your strength capacity, eye gripping and tear trenching but you hold on. Though it seems like everything you have put your hands to do is dying right before your eyes, everybody that you have some form of love for in your heart, seems as though they are disappearing from your inner circle, just hold on. God never intended us to be so troubled with the cares of this world that is why we must always keep our focus on the powers of God. Even through times of death, perhaps a dear close

Faith Without Works Are Dead. Press and PUSH ...
loved one, God does not expect us to be troubled but to place all that we have left in the inside of our heart, until it overwhelms our soul and then the troubles disappear. *Proverbs 21:1 says, "The King's heart is in the hands of the Lord, as the rivers of the water: he turneth it whithersoever he will."*

    No matter what Job lost he continued to call upon the name of the Lord, he continued to look up to the hills which his help cometh from. More than enough things that appear in our life are not recognized as faith seeds. If you ever really go through enough you will then stop giving in to failure and you will begin to look at your loss and begin to expect greater than before. Calculating a major loss and still trusting in the Lord only increases favor ability from the Lord. Regardless of how awful a situation may appear, I always like to keep my eyes remaining on just one piece of good to come out or of it. Just as an example, when hurricane Katrina came with a mighty wind prepared to destroy many evil ways and things that were going on in this world. I just say that God is God and regardless of how many tore down homes, businesses, churches and all the other destructions that occurred out of the storm, God still brought peace to many that called upon Him. No matter how much the meteorologist, weather providers and newscasters were trying to tell of the storm before it hit, unexpectedly, and did so much damage, yes,

Faith Without Works Are Dead. Press and PUSH ...

this storm left buildings, homes, businesses destroyed and many relationships that would have caused many to go down the wrong path. God just had to separate some folks in order to change some lives. When God has put out an order for your life, He will do whatever it takes just to get to that one. He knew some praying child believed in Him for a brighter future. And someone asked Him for a miracle, so many received many blessings that have set them up for the rest of their lives and then some needed to bow down because they forgot that He was God. God will have His way at any moment just to be noticed and God's plan was in place long before you and I were ever birthed. Many blessings appeared to have come out of this particular storm. Just simply think of all that have not or forgotten to call upon the name of the Lord and through this storm many hearts, minds, bodies and souls cried out to Jesus just to help them. Many want to put all their focus on the destruction of the storms but look at all the blessings that came out of Katrina's destruction. Some people were blessed with more afterwards than before. Some obtained a debt free home, better developments, and better quality of schools for their children and better Jobs. In addition, some were just disconnected from all the wrong people heading for full destruction. God needed to change some life styles, relationships and redirect some lives. God's hands covered those that opened up their hearts unto Him, and so many could

Faith Without Works Are Dead. Press and PUSH ...

not look towards the help of the government, city, state or even federal government so, therefore, they only had to depend on the hand of God. Look at the many people that looked down on the poor, homeless and the less fortunate, but for the rest of their lives, they will never look down on them again. Now they will have compassion to love them always being reminded that one day they too were once there. Storms come in all shapes and sizes; they can travel at any force of wind to tear down, abuse, hurt or wound anybody's life and it does not always matter who it hits, storms just come. In addition, when a storm flows through, if you are in the pathway of it then you too will be caught up in it; all that surround you will feel the effects of the aftermath. However, remember the power is in the storm creator, just as He allows the thunder to roar He can allow *peace in the storm. John 14:27 says, "Peace I leave with you, my peace I give unto you: not as the world giveth, give I unto you. Let not your heart be troubled, neither let it be afraid."*

You will also experience magnificent gratitude, just being appreciative for the simple things in life, such as the little things that most of us have daily and many have forgotten to show God that we appreciate Him. God allows the enemy to tempt His true servants just to strengthen them and let the enemy know that they are His. If you can overcome temptation then you are proving to God,

Faith Without Works Are Dead. Press and PUSH ...
yourself and others that you are His servant. Temptation can cause one to come up with victory, hope and gladness in their heart after the fact that they overcame. Temptation is an evil thing but once you gain the interest of overcoming it instead of gaining the interest of falling into it then you are gaining a whole new perspective on life with living in His fullness for a reward. Your heart won't be troubled anymore through failures, or weakness through temptations but will become great with appreciation which will cause you to triumph and believe greater than you had in the powers of God.

Before I began this spiritual journey in getting to know my Father who is in Heaven, I realized that I always was creative. Vision was not a problem to me but dreaming was. I had many qualifications to meet all specifications that would grow towards a certain unique quality, but I believed too much in myself, I depended too much on myself and I credited myself more than I did God. It was not intentional because I have always been a believer in God but it was not to the fullness that He wanted it to be. We must encounter the Spirit of God through a spiritual experience. You cannot see the Spirit with your eyes nor can you touch the Spirit with your hands but surely, you can feel the Spirit once the Spirit of God moves upon you. One thing about God, He is a jealous God. In addition, He just wants us to appreciate that He is.

He wants us to realize that even in the brink of a storm that He is with us. God does not want us to believe greater in ourselves than in Him, unless we are believing that it is all because of Him, that we achieved *all* due to His powers, not our own. God is awesome in the manner in which He takes care of us as we go through many life obstacles, especially as you keep your mind stayed on Him. He will lead you when your sight is gone and you cannot see, let alone find your way. God will take you by the hand and lift you out of any storm, regardless of how treacherous it is. God does not ever want us to be afraid, worried or allow fear to cancel out our peace in Him. *Job 33:29 says, "Lo, all these things worketh God oftentimes with man,"*

God loves to accept the credit for the workmanship of our hands. He loves glory and He uses the work of His people to receive glorification. Too many people for years God have been showing to the world their accomplishments, their achievements and they have received the glory for the work of God. Well, God does not like anyone to receive more glory than Him. Most of the times, He will allow us to be broken down, tempted and stripped of our personal accomplishments, just to show others and us that He is. I like to think of it as a personal spiritual reminder. After all, God will have His way whether we agree or disagree. Just as Job had to go through his temptation season of

Faith Without Works Are Dead. Press and PUSH ...

affliction to his soul, well God allowed it. However, Job had accomplished a marvelous work, accumulated much wealth and he had prospered greatly but God wanted to show him greater. More men received from Job that he was a mighty man in stature but God wanted the glory. Not saying that Job was not gracious to God but God just was not lifted enough in His life. As Job went through his suffering period, soul affliction period, torment period, lost period, and scandalizing period; he realized afterwards he had to wait on the Lord. Sometimes, we are so used to doing things ourselves until God will remind us we must be patient. Sometimes in life, we can achieve so much in material but so little in true faith. God feels the need to rearrange the way we perceive just who He really is. As the work of your hands will begin to unfold, give God all the credit. After all, if the Lord were not on your side then where would you be? How can your work really speak for Him? *1 Samuel 16:7 says, "But the Lord said unto Samuel. Look not on his countenance or on the height of His stature; because I have refused him: for the Lord seeth not as man seeth; for man looketh on the outward appearance, but the Lord looketh on the heart."*

However, Job had great vision and accomplished greatly in his visions through his life's work but God desired more of Him just as He desires more of you. Through the work of your

Faith Without Works Are Dead. Press and PUSH ...
hands, others are able to see who you are. The work of your hands will always give others an impression about you. Your hands will show if you are a persistent person or just the opposite. The work of your hands will speak either of yourself or because of the God you serve. Just as Job had great determination to achieve, God used Him for a greater way to speak too many just as you and I. Job suffered greatly through His trying times, through his tribulations and through his temptations as the enemy sat there and had the authority from God to tempt him. Regardless of what we all go through time and time again, we must keep our focus/ability on God. Many things will appear in your life but it is all appearing just for a purpose of righteousness, God is justifying you in Him. He is making things appear in your life so that He can build up a fruitful spirit in you. Without longsuffering then you will never understand patience, without trying times you will never get to know unspeakable peace. Without stormy situations then you will never have the opportunity to say, peace is still in my life. Often times we gain much of the world but very little in spirit, God wants to grip the chambers of your heart. He wants to be that blood that pumps through each vain or vessel of your body to interlock each of the four chambers of your heart so that you will know that it is nobody but the Lord, and not you yourself. As men and women look upon you, God wants them to see His glimmering light shining on you. Without

Faith Without Works Are Dead. Press and PUSH ...

being in a bad situation going through much acquisition then how could God ever dispense the pleasure of His goodness upon your life? In addition, all those tears that have fallen down the cheeks of your face and staying up in agony all night long, joy would be impossible for your morning time. Without everything seeming to look impossible through your eyesight then how could God ever build your faith not through your sight but through heart application of His word? Understand that no matter what you gain of this world, without feeling His magnificent Spirit of the Holy Ghost then how can you truly say that you have felt the touch of the Lord? God loves to astound us with His specialty of performing another miracle in our lives. He just wants to inhabit His fruitfulness in your life through His spirit. If you do not ever experience a moment of unhappiness then how can you have a true reason to laugh and understand the reason for happiness? *Matthew 18:4 says, "Whosoever therefore shall humble himself as this little child, the same is greatest in the kingdom of heaven."*

God is just developing some supernatural things in your life that your money just could not seem to buy. Job was a very rich man, well to do, good personality and possessed great qualities for a magnificent role model to many but God needed to justify Job's life. If your spirit was always calm through everything, then how could you ever have

Faith Without Works Are Dead. Press and PUSH ...
the opportunity of handling your situations with meekness? And as the rocky situations occur in your life that sometimes try to cause you to lose your mind, being in a desperate situation, then how could you ever look forward to getting to know God's gentleness. I know you want to see this thing work out in your life and I know you feel it with all sensation of coming truth; God is just reminding you of who He is in a very personal way. God wants a one on one personal relationship with you. In order for Him to get what He wants, He will make some things happen in your life to bring you out of your familiarity zone. Today is your comfort zone alteration time. He does not like it when we depend so greatly on ourselves, on our loves ones, on our friends or on our works of achievements because He wants us to solely depend on Him for greatness in return. Just as Job got tired of feeling so much agony, pain and hurt until he wondered why? He felt as though he deserved none of it because of the life without sin that he lived. I have felt that many times. I have cried to God tears that could never be counted and that I will never forget. The pain and hurt that I had to go through almost made me lose my soul. It hurts especially when you know you have been faithful, determined, trying till you've given everything you got and still no answer; still no change in your situation. There are many times that I have given, and just absolutely went overboard trying to be a blessing but still I felt that there was

no change. When God is working on you, He works in wondrous ways. Ways that you do not always get an immediate answer but He is working it out just for you.

God Is Just Building up Your Trust.

Job 29:1 says, moreover Job continued his parable, and said,
Job 29:2 Oh that I were as in months past, as in the days when God preserved me;

You are not alone going through your problems. Just as God was with Job, He is here with you. As we sometimes get so comfortable in our lives and things are finally going wonderfully, then it just seems like all hell will break loose. I want you to know, as hell is breaking loose in your life, in your vision God is binding it up. Though it is painful and yes it hurts, do not let it ruin your faith because this is your faith building time. As I look back even during the time I was writing this book and had put so much work effort in the church it just seemed like all hell broke loose. Just as the church was developing, I thought to its fullness, it suddenly closed up. I know I had been very faithful, taking things in life and sucking it up. I would not even let the ones that I thought I could always depend on hurt me as they all turned their backs on me. It appears the very ones that you so diligently work

Faith Without Works Are Dead. Press and PUSH ...

for, pray for and try to instruct are the very ones that will hurt you the most as you go through. My old familiar saying is, "If you really want to know who is on your side then take a hard fall down and look up, tell me who you see?" At this time I had given up my business to be more available to work in the ministry full time, sold many valuables to access funds for the church to be in operation and much fasting and praying. I poured out everything I had to prove to the members just how serious I was about desiring to teach the word. I thought I had proven my love to God and that I was serious and I often times quoted many scriptures trying to get God to show up immediately in an emergency. Eventually, the property owner could not hold out any longer and the eviction notice was served without me being properly notified. Then on top of all that the notice was mailed to an unknown address that I no longer occupied, just so I would not receive the notification on time. It is a hurting thing when you know you are doing all that you can. After all, my husband and I had to hire help because not one member showed up to help us move out of the building. I felt that all was for nothing because the very people I expected to be by our sides were nowhere to be found. Again, God will take you out of your comfort zone; he loves rearranging even your surroundings. I had people in my corner just as Job that I thought would be with me at my time of need. All those years I had a business I could always look up and see them

Faith Without Works Are Dead. Press and PUSH ...

trying to help me, so they said. All the times the church was in operation, many ran to help or to see how they could assist me. It's a beautiful thing when trouble comes your way because through your troubling times you'll really notice who is there for you. It's really a heart breaker when the ones you thought would be praying with you; you only wanted to say, I knew they weren't who they claimed to be but they forgot all about who Job was and the God I serve. Just because you could be going through do not worry about what folks say about you. Who cares if no one on this earth wants to see you make it, just hold on as God reveals Himself in your life through the works of HIS hands? God took Job out of his comfort zone and out of the comfort of his normal association just to speak to him through a young man that he did not know that well. It's awesome how God will send someone your way to be by your side to encourage you to the greater. My life was a setup, the ministry was a setup and my future was a setup. Oh, how they laughed at me and my husband. So many had been waiting on the day to come when I failed, and oh how I cried with the way so many hurt me. I cried out for the last time in that way.

Things Are Going To Get Better

If he could feel the presence of God watching over him as he used to, oh how much better life

Faith Without Works Are Dead. Press and PUSH ...
could be. I too sat and thought, maybe I should have kept my beauty salon or maybe I should have worked even harder in the church; maybe if this or maybe that had happened is not going to make it better. If so, then it all would have happened that way. Then the more I wrote, the more God spoke to me and He said, "There was no more that you could do - now it's my time to do it." Think about that. Just as you tried all that you could, now you have no more. Just as you gave all that you had and you cannot give any more, it is just time for God to do it, because he has taken it all out of your hands. It is God's time to speak. Through that period of no more Fountains, I realized that God wanted greater. I thought I had a great vision before but guess what, it grew even larger. Even the love for the ones that loved seeing me in my predicament grew it greater. I refused to allow man the upper hand in my life; I realized that I wanted to trust God more. Often times, as we think we really know God well, we do not always know him as we think we do. God made me write more and more each day and he told me that it all was a set up. I had to give it all up, so that he could make time for the gift of writing that He has placed in my heart. He had to close the doors of the church just so that He could open up the doors for *The House of Transformation Miracle Ministries*. God is a God of justification; He will take any situation and make it right. Job's life was a set up to look like he had fallen without God on His

Faith Without Works Are Dead. Press and PUSH ...

side. People talked about him, laughed and ridiculed him, even joked about the God he served, tried to get him to curse his God and die. Though Job complained, as he reminisced greatly on his past and though he felt every bit of his pain, he still was in the hands of God. No matter what his life appeared then too many, God never took his hand off Job. I do not care what it is that you are going through no one can turn that thing around in your life but God. Do not expect great things from folks especially when you serve a God that is the definition of Excellency.

People tried to put Job in many different unfaithful character classifications but it all just could not be, because God was justifying him. Right now, your life has definitely been set up, just as Job. You are now set up to gain trust from God that is going to make your last fruit be made whole in the love manifestation of the LORD. This set up is like no other because it is going to make many wonderful great things and great people come your way, just to bless you. Your entire future is going to be definitely changed due to the fact of this set up. Trusting in God is going to be so worthy until it will be made available to pay off any amount of wealth worth in your life. This was a set up for every door that has been shut is now going to be opened; it all is a set up. God is establishing you with a worth to fully inherit substance of things you never knew that

Faith Without Works Are Dead. Press and PUSH ...

you would gain. He is now going to trust you with greater things in life, greater vision to add to your vision and greater people are going to be by your side to help you make it. This trust is a lifelong lasting dependability on Him because of the hope, patience, faith, love, longsuffering, meekness, gentleness, temperance, joy and happiness that He is going to incorporate in your life. It is a trust that cannot be revoked; it is an incorruptible trust that is guaranteed to pay the full benefits of a life long-standing annuity insurance policy. If something happens to you, then it will automatically trigger down to the next of kin and so on. You will know longer have to worry about things in your life because through this trust every vision that God has given you shall speak and many shall see it. Just hold on and remain faithful, hold on and wait on the Lord He is just finishing up your paper work. See all those that went against Job, it was all a set up for you to gain the Trust of God. Though that work in your hands may look worthless right now believe me there is going to be a payday so expect it. That day is closer now of being finished than you first thought. Your hands are going to speak of the powers of God without your mouth having to say a word just because of the works He is about to do in your life, it's all just been a set up. *Job 32:18 says, "For I am full of matter, the spirit within me constraineth me."*

Faith Without Works Are Dead. Press and PUSH ...
It was hard for Job to understand why he was going through so much. Three of his friends came by to see of him but none of them could answer him conclusively. Job continued with his entire saying but still no truth could be brought forth as he analyzed all his righteousness seeing no wrong. Nevertheless, in the midst God was standing there with this young fellow Elihu, he had been compelled with God and full of the Spirit of God. Elihu was very angry as he listened to Job and his friends speak on Job's situation. He had become angry as Job spoke on all his righteousness other than the righteousness of God. God wanted to put Job's house in the correct order. Moreover, God had sent Elihu to be his representative to give great word instruction. See, anyone couldn't just get Job's attention, it had to be a designated person that was full of the wisdom of God and knew something of Job's experiences of going through in order to receive Job's full attention on the matter. Just as myself, I had to learn to speak to God and ask him to have his way in my life.

At times, we all have the tendency to think that we know things and sometimes we want to believe we know it all because we feel that we are right. Well, our righteousness is not the same as God's righteousness. Things that look clear to bring us a certain understanding is not always the same understanding as God's understanding. God has a

Faith Without Works Are Dead. Press and PUSH ...
magnificent way to mold our real understanding into shape by giving it a full personality effect that will impact many non-believers and will make them become believers. It is that creativeness that God can get many to notice just who He really is, He loves to get attention and He will use force to do so. His force is powerful and it will restrain you in position to receive all that He has designated just for your life. God knows so much of what He wants for us even down to who He wants us to network with which is amazing. However, all of His affects are amazing and through them all, He receives full attention through the spirit.

As Elihu spoke they heard the force of the voice of the Lord, he spoke with power and with pure confidence because he truly knew of the Lord. He was one that declared the spirit of the Lord had made him. God wants us made not by words alone but spiritually, that is the true word connection that will produce faith in your lives. It guarantees power when you need quick accessibility and for sureness where doubt would try to surface. Faith inhabits righteousness while at the same time causes the enemy to flee from you. Elihu was not at all concerned with what had happened to Job or with what he had lost, he was fully concerned with giving God great creditability through any situation. He stressed to Job the great works and wonders of God, he wanted Job to look upon all the powers that

Faith Without Works Are Dead. Press and PUSH ...
God has, not his situation. Elihu wanted Job to really see that God is faithful with working wonders. Immediately, after Elihu had spoken, then God stepped in with His words to answer Job, reminding him of whom He was as he created this earth and everything in it; gave him some details. God continued speaking to Job and after Job responded to God through humbling himself, God then rebuked his three friends that added to Job's suffering. According to Job as recorded in the 42nd chapter and 41st verse, I believe that God mightily blessed Elihu for standing in on his behalf with such faithful words of wisdom as he had given Job. I know one day I was going through so much in my life with my marriage, yes preachers have marriage problems just like everyone else, and I will never forget one of my dear friends in the Lord said to me, "God has given you a particular Anointing just for your husband." Lord that was the truth because He had. So many things, so many trials and so many questions - don't worry about it or them, just stay focused on all you know that God is capable of doing in your life. Your hand personality is a weapon for the enemy because as you continue the works in faith through your hands, God is going to give you greater anointing powers. He is going to give you powers in the works of your hands until they will be a mighty force for Him. After all the facts had been brought to Job's attention and he came to full realization and humbled himself, all He

Faith Without Works Are Dead. Press and PUSH...

had was restored double for all of his troubles. God knows all that you are really worth that is why He gives us gain. Though Job apparently thought he had it all, God knew of his great reward before he first went into his suffering season. Just as the work of your hands as you continue to work on finishing your vision; your reward is going to be humungous. *Proverbs 8:1 says, doth not wisdom cry? And understanding put forth her voice?*

Just as Elihu appeared to Job not a man of pure word such as his other friends, family and neighborhood companions but as a faithful person to God through it all. This young fellow was tender in years but full with spiritual wisdom through spiritual experience. I can imagine that as Elihu spoke he spoke words with a powerful force that changed Job's destiny because he spoke words of life. He was full with all that mattered to the God that he knew he served. He was not one without knowledge but one with great words of wisdom. He inspired Job as he told Job of the powerful things that God had carried him through. In addition, most likely Elihu had gone through greater tribulation than Job that is why he was able to speak so richly of God. He knew all that Job was experiencing but he knew greater of his own triumph through him remaining faithful to God through it all. As he told Job God had constrained him that means that God had also caused him to be bound down on a bed of

Faith Without Works Are Dead. Press and PUSH ...
seeming not to ever get back up. God will lock some things in his chosen peoples' lives just to disconnect them from the way they have formally first believed in him. God is a God of power that will force the wrong out just to force the right in. Look at your hands, those hands are created in the same manner, they shall produce with a force. Your hands are going to connect you to the things in this life to bless you eternally with all of his preciousness. Elihu only trusted God so because he knew of the works of God. As God begins forcing some things out of your life that does not have enough life of him in it, then he is going to force some things in it to produce righteousness. Elihu once lost greatly but he too was not a gainer of just wealth, health and prosperity but a gainer of the fullness of the Lord. He was made through the spiritual enrichment of God's forceful power. Elihu was anointed with powers to speak and as he spoke, immediately, Job's destiny begin to shake. It shook so until God was about to then answer Job and Job was able to receive it all through humbling himself. God caused Elihu to be there on time for Job to introduce His force of powers and wondrous works in a manner that they have never heard of or received. By the time Elihu finished Job could say nothing but yes Lord, he was able to acknowledge that God was just having his way in his life and he knew then that God wouldn't dare leave him incomplete. *Philippians 2:8 says, "And being found in fashion as a man, he*

Faith Without Works Are Dead. Press and PUSH ...
humbled himself, and became obedient unto death, even the death of the cross."

We serve a God that gives humungous gifts, gifts so large until they will cause an overflow of blessings. As your faith through your humbleness is made complete unto God then He will restore some things that you thought you lost in your life. Actually, start adding it up now of all that you have lost for all your times of troubles and expect double in return. Yes, God set Job up not to prove his faithfulness but to bless Him with a double reward. See, many people were already noticing all of Job's valuables and the worth but after his huge lost now they was able to see greater worth, greater valuables, greater things, humungous substance, and his inheritance because of his faithfulness unto God. When people look upon Job's worth today, they are not noticing as much as his gain because all they see before anything is Faith. They notice his faith in God, they knew that he waited on God and you to with patience just wait on the Lord, He'll do it all for you. Now let your hands work with a personality that can produce others to become faithful in God, all your hands to be characterized as hands with anointing power. Let people see that it is God working in you, through you and you are because He is. Allow your work to be noticed with the fruitfulness of the Spirit of God. Just as God set Job

Faith Without Works Are Dead. Press and PUSH ...
up, He has also set you up to bless your life and to sanctify your future with unfailing hope.

The Anointing Power of your Hands

CHAPTER 8

Figuring Out Your Faith

Proverbs 3:5, says, *"Trust in the Lord with all thine heart; and lean not unto thine own understanding."* God has spoken to you and He has given you a commission. Perhaps more than once you have heard His voice but now it is time to listen. Moreover, you heard Him as He whispered to you. Many times, you have dreamed of your life being everything you ever hoped for. Then you woke up still stuck in your life. Often saying, what if this dream was true? Hoping that you could live that dream. Sometimes feeling that you would be better off if you had never awakened. Surely we all have felt that way one time or another, especially when we cannot handle the pressures of life. Many things have appeared in our lives that we did not

Faith Without Works Are Dead. Press and PUSH ...

expect. Life crisis has thrown you off guard and the way your life appears was nowhere in your life plans. Things happened to you without notice and many times, you actually wished your life were the dream that you had been dreaming. *It seems as though many of us have been marked to be destroyed.* Moreover, none of this was supposed to happen to you, but it did. Nevertheless, still no real proof of your dreams coming to reality. Perhaps, you have tried and you may have tried in many ways. Still nothing seems to have worked out. You want a better life but how bad do you desire it? Your hopes soon turn to dreams and your dreams soon turned into a brief moment of happiness, until you wake up. Sometimes your mind has drifted into your dream world, hoping for this dream to come true. Moreover, doubt begins to laugh in your face and surfaces in your mind, now your dreams are cancelled out. Your hopes are now hopeless and there is no desperation causing you to continue to hope for your dreams to be true. However, you wanted it all to happen, growing up with many great expectations for your life, but your life has seemed to go down the drain. I am here to tell you that you need this vision to work, do not quit hoping for it now. Find you some new hope and let your new hope cause your dreams to come true. If God did it for me, He too can do it for you. The key is no matter what happened in my life, I never stopped dreaming. I never gave up and I was not prepared to

Faith Without Works Are Dead. Press and PUSH ...

let anything stop me. Slam on the gas and get off the brakes, let your dreams accelerate. You need it to be real. Let your effort push you forward. Your life destiny is depending on it. You want it and you have tried in every way, but did you give it all you had? Did you push yourself into God's Anointing Powers? When you reach the depths of His powers then your vision will speak boldly. His Anointing will prosper your vision. Increase will flow into operation. I want you to understand this one thing, only you can cause it to come forth. If you do not desire it strong enough then God does not have to let it happen. Perhaps your dreams were not large enough to cause Him to move on your behalf. However, He intentionally wanted you to believe in Him for a miracle that is going to forever affect the way you think of Him. Dreams are in a world of its own but reality is what you live in. Let God bring your dreams into reality. No matter how large your dreams are, remember, God will give you your heart's desires. If you desire it then it is yours, if you believe that He is able then it is already done and if you know Him, then what are you still doing dreaming? God is a God of prosperity and He lives to purposely cause the dead to rise in Him. Get more God. All you have to do is delight yourself in Him. *Psalms 37:4 says, Delight thyself also in the Lord, and he shall give thee the desires of thine heart.*

Faith Without Works Are Dead. Press and PUSH...

Just think about all the things that you will be able to do, with the Anointing Powers of God working in your hands. If you really use what He has blessed you with you will receive The Anointing. You will have the power to do anything you set your mind to do. It does not matter how big your dreams are. God has the power to bring them all to reality. It does not matter if you have multiple visions. I mean enough to fill the largest football stadium in the world. It can happen for you. It does not matter if your dreams are great enough to fill a whole city or even the world. This is an example of how large God wants your heart's desire to be in Him. Your dreams will only live through the faith that you have in The Powers of God. If you think small, you will only believe a little in Him. Get over that mustard seed of faith and let your faith grow up in Him. God wants to develop your faith, as He will cause it to mature. Allow Him to manifest everything within your life. Let Him give you hope that will cause you to gain more life. As you gain a greater life then many others will survive off of your hope. It is time to realize the depth and to know the many life opportunities that will live just because of your dreams. God has the power for you to do it all. How many lives can be affected through the reality of your dreams? The work of your hands is going to affect many to be encouraged in Him or discouraged. Your hands possess powers but which powers do they currently possess? Are they

Faith Without Works Are Dead. Press and PUSH...
affecting lives to desire Him more or are they canceling out someone else's faith? Sometimes our dreams do not come true because God is not finished showing us the whole dream. Other times, it is because our hearts are not finished growing in Him. He wants The Power of Love to work through our hands. He wants someone else to be connected to Him through our works. He wants our lives to speak that He is real and to know that He lives. You need spiritual motivation; it is the only possibility for you to achieve all the visions He has given you. The Anointing can do it all. It is just waiting on you. I am one that knows about vision. I too have had many. I have had so many someone once said, "Do you think you are trying to do too much at one time?" At first, I thought I did, but it was my many dreams that kept me running forward. Apparently, I was, but I believed so much in the word of God and I knew He gave them all to me so I was not prepared to put one vision on the back burner. Soon afterwards, Jamie Fox appeared on The Oprah Show - a very gifted man in many ways. He said, "You can do it all." Looking back over his many accomplishments, I realized if he could then so can I. He is one with many talents and has been a great achiever in many ways. Remember, if someone else can then so can you. Though you think your dreams are too big for you they are just right for God to bless them to come forth.

Faith Without Works Are Dead. Press and PUSH ...
Every vision that God has given you is for a purpose, to bring you out in many ways. He wants you to put your hands on it. My visions helped saved my life. I simply needed them all. I begin to work in every angle I could in order to achieve. They all lifted my spirits and kept me motivated in Him. Many times, I wanted to give up but I could not. When God gives you a vision it is made to be spiritual. His Spirit saved my life repeatedly and the many visions caused me to run on. Every song, book, business and vision for the ministry was God's way of giving me hope. God wants you to hold on and move forward in your life. Things will get better. Actually, they will be so good at times that you will begin to burst out and just laugh. God has a mighty way of making us laugh without anything being funny. His love is different and it is beyond words I cannot express it but it is wonderful. *Proverbs 22:6 says, Train up a child in the way he should go: and when He is old, he will not depart from it.*

If it was not for the many visions God has given me, I often wondered where my children's destiny would be. Our children suffer as we do. They too feel the many pressures of life. Often parents do not realize the agony we put our children through. The same way you feel your life is in a mess is the same way they feel too. God knew I needed my visions, because they kept inspiring me to live. They also gave my children hope and caused them to believe more in Him. I wanted God to know that I appreciated every gift, talent and vision He had given me. I ran with them all because each vision served its own purpose. Know that your dreams serve a purpose not only to give life but also, to save lives. As you will begin to let The Anointing flow through your hands, God will bring your needs forth. As I continued my children were inspired and as they saw me achieve they too begin to gain vision. The Anointing Powers of your hands will simply connect someone else with greater hope. Allow God to work through you and then He will begin to work through your children. As a parent, I wanted to train my children to believe that God is real. I wanted them to carry on in my footsteps as I taught them to fear Him by *simply teaching them the right from the wrong.* We must let God Anoint the works of our hands so that our children can grow up knowing that The Anointing is real. The best way to teach someone is to show him or her the way. Show your children that The Anointing is in you. Teach them to desire The Anointing Powers of God through the way you live. Children live by our lifestyles. What way are you showing your child? Whatever you are, they too will become, teach them that the impossibilities are possible.

You must know that you are a visionary. A dreamer only has dreams but a visionary reaches their destiny. The Anointing Powers of God will work in you. He wants you to put your hands to work on the vision He has giving you. Only you can desire it in your heart until God will have to allow it to come forth. Put your hands to work and God will anoint them. He will give you the power and your vision shall speak for itself. Lay your hands on it, as God will surge His Anointing Powers through you. *Genesis 1:27 says, So God created man in His own image, in the image of God created he him; male and female created he them.*

God has given you a perfect hand design. The majority of jobs require you to apply yourself with hands on training. Without your hands, makes it almost impossible to work at any average job. So many have what it takes and will not use what God has given them. You must allow the precious blood of The Anointing to flow through your fingertips. They will do a wonderful work and many others will notice. Without you putting your hands on it, then what good are your gifts? I know many people with beautiful voices that will sing your socks off but they'd rather work a job paying minimum wage. Many people have God given gifts but they will not trust God enough to get them out of a life of poverty. They have sacrificed their future as well as their children's future because of their lack of courage. You must be prepared to show the world what you have working on the inside of you. Show

Faith Without Works Are Dead. Press and PUSH ...

them how The Power of God is in you. Let Him perform a marvelous work as you put your hands on it. I know just as God created this earth He was excited about the beauty thereof. He wanted someone to glorify His works. God created us so that He can be glorified. Let Him be glorified through you. We all notice how powerful God really is after seeing Him work mightily in another. Let The Anointing Powers in your hands show the world how large God is in you. *John 20:27 says, Then saith he to Thomas, Reach hither thy finger, and behold my hands; and reach hither thy hand, and thrust it into my side: and be not faithless, but believing.*

God has heavenly powers ready to anoint the works of your hands. He loves to anoint us because He gains more glory. When you realize the power that is in God, you will know it is available to you too. He created us in His imagine and He created us to be all-powerful. Let Him begin to flourish His anointing powers through you. Let Him grow larger in you. Put no limits on how large God will expand Himself in you. Just note, as He grows larger in you then He will be magnified through your children. I do not see God begging for anything and neither should His children. Everything that God wants is instantly done. God does not have a need, what about you? Know that The Anointing is real and powerful things will happen once The Anointing

Faith Without Works Are Dead. Press and PUSH ...
surfaces in you. Just as our children reap from our benefits, a child of God reaps from Him. Whatever you need, God He has it and if you want it, He will give it to you. In order for God to allow the anointing power to be accepted into your life, you must give up things of this world and walk in God's spirit. Remember, you can only serve one God at a time. When you really mean business and you have a vision, some things must change in your life. Get busy in your vision. God created you to be powerful, so therefore you need to indulge yourself in Him. His Anointing is purposed for us to receive power and daily we should show Him appreciation. You have to know the One you love. After all, it is He that possesses the powers to get you to your life's destiny. Without God then we would not exist. In addition, without His anointing in my life, I would have never received the Anointing Powers of my hands. I thank God for His anointing because it has brought forth many beautiful things in my life. The things that God placed in my heart and the joy that He brings forth will cause one to be filled with daily happiness. Worldly things cannot compare to the peace of His serenity. I imagine that Thomas pointed out the doubts that were in his heart with his hands. You must decide if you are going to continue allowing your life to stay this way or if you are going to put forth, reach higher and receive The Anointing. The Anointing will flow through your fingers causing you to gain a surge of the

Faith Without Works Are Dead. Press and PUSH ...

magnificent heavenly powers. They will work mightily through your hands.

John 20:27 says, Then saith he to Thomas, Reach hither thy finger, and behold my hands; and reach hither thy hand, and thrust it into my side: and be not faithless, but believing.

This man named Thomas was also known to many to be "Doubting Thomas," a name that followed him because of his times of doubting the truth about Jesus. Moreover, he *reached* the point of truth by touching Jesus. Thomas was one considered to always doubt until the truth was made known unto him. Though he had known of God, he was not sure about Jesus. Even being one of the twelve disciples, Thomas believed in absolutely none of his friend's own words. Thomas wanted true clarity. He was one that believed through seeing and touching for himself. No one could tell him anything. He simply had to see it to be true with his own eyes. He did not have faith. That is exactly why the generations today are going astray because many have raised their children without knowing Jesus. Though many people know God, so they say they have no faith in Jesus. They can believe that God created the world in a few days and caused Noah to build an ark but they do not accept that JESUS rose up with all power in His hands. Jesus has all the power. He is *The Descender*.

Faith Without Works Are Dead. Press and PUSH ...

I **know** only one way that many would not take the word of a friend. It is either that you do not know them that well or that you do not trust him or her. Thomas was known as The Doubter. A doubter is an unbeliever and he or she is one, which needs convincing. I concluded that he never truly knew Jesus because he did not trust that He was the Messiah. Once you know Jesus, there is no turning back. No one in his or her right frame of mind would want to be separated from Jesus because of His greatness. His love is full of compassion and once you taste His flavor, you will never let Him go. Yes, I was a doubter too before I knew Him. However, now that I know Him I could not live without Him. He has changed my life and has given it a new meaning. Life without Him is impossible to live a life of goodness. Thomas needed to touch Him for himself. *Jeremiah 29:13 says, "And ye shall seek me, and find me, when ye shall search for me with all your heart."*

Sometimes we make life more complicated when we do not search for the truth. It is either that we are simply lazy or do not want to do our own research. Often times, we just have the wrong **resources**. Faith grows as we decide to reach for it. We must put our priorities in order. First, Thomas needed to put His finger through the wounds of Jesus before He would believe. He wanted to know

Faith Without Works Are Dead. Press and PUSH ...

the truth for himself that Jesus was the Messiah. Many criticized Thomas for doubting. Just as people may criticize you today, do not let it stop you. He had to touch Jesus because he wanted to feel Him. Most people would have just taken their friend's advice, but not Thomas. Many people are too trusting; they will trust anyone and anything. I know there were many times people told me things but nothing in my life changed until I touched Jesus for myself. You have to delight yourself in Him until you press yourself into His Anointing. The presence of Jesus is powerful but the touch of Him is more powerful. It is Anointing. Yes, I saw many things in my life and I felt His presence many times. However, when I begin to reach forth and touched Him for myself, Jesus Anointed me. It does not matter who you are, where you have been in life and what you are not, He has the power to Anoint. No yoke, stronghold or even you can stop yourself once The Anointing comes upon you. God wants your work to be anointed. He wants it to be a powerful work and wants you to lay your hands on Him. Thomas never gave in to what they said; neither did he care what anyone thought of him.

Often times too many people are quick to run with what they hear than what they know. Thomas was smart; I must say He wanted to feel Jesus for himself. Thomas was prepared to do what was necessary to find the truth for himself. He did not

Faith Without Works Are Dead. Press and PUSH ...

want to trust any of the disciples. In many similar cases people will allow what they have seen or heard to stop their beliefs. Thomas was one that made sure no one was going to stop him from finding out the truth. Just because some of the other disciples were probably not what he would have expected them to be, they did not stop him from figuring out the truth. Regardless of your feelings towards another that professes the gospels, do not let it stop you. That is the key focus why so many visions are buried today, they allow what someone else says destroy their dreams. I have heard so many people say that is why I do not go to church. All because of what someone else has done. Do not let what others do, think or say stop you. After all, it will only ruin your life. One saying I love to say, "If someone wants to play with their life then let them but I will not play with mine." *John 20:27 says, "Then saith he to Thomas, Reach hither thy finger, and behold my hands; and reach hither thy hand, and thrust it into my side: and be not faithless, but believing."*

Thomas put his fingers through Jesus' wounds. It inspired Thomas' faith to go deep. Once he touched Jesus, He was a believer. His faith grew through the wounds of Jesus. Thomas was more than just inspired, He felt The Anointing flowing through His fingertips. Once you begin to touch Jesus as you reach forth, you will feel The Almighty presence of God move through you. God wants your hands to reach up to Him. He wants to anoint you and give you Power. The key to reaching up is that you aim high. He is The Highest of the High. He wants you to aim for the height of your life. He wants to give you all of your heart's desires including your major dreams. *John 20:27 says, "Then saith he to Thomas, Reach hither thy finger, and behold my hands; and reach hither thy hand, and thrust it into my side: and be not faithless, but believing."*

Often many do not reach God in the manner He wants us to. You must look up, aim high and feel His Anointing. Stop letting people and excuses stop you from reaching The Anointing. It is powerful. I was once in a conversation with one of my clients. She said, "It does not take all of that shouting, jumping and stuff to praise or worship God." To some maybe no but for me yes it did. Once I felt Jesus for myself, I could not sit there as though I felt nothing. He is powerful and once you "really" feel The Anointing, you will never be the same. I used to go to church like I was sitting on a log and I sat on my blessings. I would hardly clap my hands or stomp my feet and my life did not change. I went to church wanting to receive but often I did not. When I realized I had to become a partaker in praise, fellowship and worship then I begin to receive a new part of the life He had purposed for me. As

Faith Without Works Are Dead. Press and PUSH ...
they say, when the praises go up the blessings come down and I needed them all. I was not a shouter or a worshiper; I was just a bench warmer. However, when that day came, I stopped sitting and I begin to praise. One day I was no longer worried about if my hair would fall or if my heels would curl over, who cares. I went in expecting a miracle and I came out with a bigger reward. God moves as we move and He works as we work. Eventually, I realized my praise grew stronger and so did I. My shouts grew louder and so did His voice. The Anointing is too much to sit down on; it will cause you to move. When The Anointing is on you there will be no room for doubt. You need the power of God to move in you, on you and to accomplish anything greater than you. I never forgot my first feeling of the Anointing. It immediately consumed everything out of me that caused me to doubt Him. The Anointing is the most powerful presence you could ever feel and it will soothe your soul.

His fingertip is what stirred up his faith. Because as he pushed himself towards the wounds of Jesus. He stretched forth his hands and inserted them through Jesus wounds. He received the power of The Anointing. He felt sure with his hands that canceled out all his doubt. The pressing, the point, the tip of his fingers plunged into The Anointing. Jesus' wounds has caused many to be saved, delivered and powered up. Finally, Thomas was

Faith Without Works Are Dead. Press and PUSH ...

able to see with his eyes and feel the precious blood of Jesus flowing through his fingertips. When you feel Jesus, you will know the purpose of His wounds. The tip of your fingers will begin to transfer the powers of God in your life. I love it as I feel my way through because the eye seeing will sometimes miss-lead you. God is a Spirit. We should look for Him to appear to us in a spiritual manner. You cannot see The Spirit but you will feel Him. However, once The Anointing comes upon you there will be no sitting still. Thomas just wanted to feel the supreme presence of the Lord for himself. As he pushed his finger, Thomas was instantly delivered. The more you press the sooner you will feel The Anointing. This press is up to how bad you desire a true heart change in your life. Your heart must feel it and you must press towards it. In your press is your reward. Know that God's rewards are forever lasting, they will never die. Seek after the things of Heaven and all the powers you will ever need. It will be right there in the palm of your hands. If you want it then push your way through until you press your way into His Anointing. Your future is in your press and The Anointing is waiting on your push.

<u>God ALMIGHTY has been waiting on you to arrive.</u>

The Anointing Power of your Hands

CHAPTER 9

Allowing the Milk & Honey to Flow in Your Life

Joel 3:18 says, *"And it shall come to pass in that day, that the mountains shall drop down new wine, and the hills shall flow with milk, and all the rivers of Judah shall flow with waters, and a fountain shall come forth of the house of the Lord, and shall water the valley of Shittim."* Have you ever sat back to think about your land flowing with milk and honey? Imagine a whole land truly flowing with milk and honey, what a sight that would be. Not only would it be a sight for your eyes to see but imagine no more struggles or major challenges to overcome. The milk in your land will be strength for your backbone because of the many challenges you would have overcome. Remember, The Anointing

God ALMIGHTY has been waiting on you to arrive.

Powers are in your hands. Your faith will be enlarged and the only way to get there is to use what God has given you. Everything in your life will be made to sweetness; there will be no turning back. God has a land just like this only for His chosen, the ones that are prepared to reach for His Glory. The winner will win it all and God wants you in that land. God created victorious winners not losers. He wants to give you increase and overflow your land with every need. Surely, you have heard this repeatedly, living in your land flowing with milk and honey. Nevertheless, have you really thought about it? I know your eyes are picturing milk draining in your land. However, picture this, heavenly power flowing in your land, no more lack or slack. When you need something, there will be no more waiting - it will just be there before you even ask. Say good-bye to suffering and Hallelujah to peace forever. I know you have sometimes heard it preached before, but have you ever meditated on it? God is speaking of your land, not your lot, your neighborhood or community but your land. Have you ever thought about it, needing no more money, lacking nothing else anymore and everywhere you turn you see His goodness and feel true happiness. I am not speaking of greed but of everything in your life to be made whole. God did not create His children to suffer, knowing that He has All-Power. He wants to bless you to live in His Supernatural Abundance. God is authentic and He has the power

<u>God ALMIGHTY has been waiting on you to arrive.</u> to make anything happen, just for you. You know how sometimes you want to go shopping but cannot because you do not have the money. Instead, you go window-shopping. What about the times you want to just pay your bills on time but instead you have to make arrangements because you do not have the money. Perhaps the times you have been laid off work and the anxiety kicks in. Stress will accumulate in your life, as it will try to attack your health. God does not expect His children to live in fear neither in lack. Just as He has all power, He expects us to. It is time to use what God has given you, so you can be increased. You have the power right there in your hands if you use them according to His will. God wants us all to live in His Eternal Blessings, meaning it starts right now and then will last forever. *Joel 3:9 says, Proclaim ye this among the Gentiles; Prepare war, wake up the mighty men, let all the men of war draw near; let them come up.*

If I do not know anything else, I know God expects us to fight for what we want. When you begin to fight for what you want you will have a determination to win. There will be a strategic plan to conquer anyone and anything working against you. In addition, you will know your enemies; the ones that do not want you to make it because you might do better than them. Nevertheless, the things that are holding you back and keeping you down. In most cases, it is sad but we are our worst enemy.

God ALMIGHTY has been waiting on you to arrive.
The enemy that lives inside you is holding you down more than anyone and anything else in your life. I say this because times I have personally caused myself not to achieve. Perhaps sometimes during my lazy spells I could not achieve anything but I most definitely gave a good talk. However, one day I decided to stop allowing myself to be held back. I had to begin to push as I prayed and prayed as I pushed in order to move forward. As long as I gave myself excuses, lived in a spirit of laziness and procrastinated I could not move ahead. This war is going to take seriousness, a mind made up and a determination to come out as a victorious winner. You must recognize your state of position in mind to know where you are going in life. Know what you want in life. In order for you to reach your land flowing with milk and honey, you must have a backing. Let the Anointing Powers of Your Hands cause God to bring you out. Let His word motivate you to move forward and let His words Anoint the works of your hands. Daily speak a powerful word to your hands. *Joel 2:12 says, "Therefore also now, saith the Lord, turn ye even to me with all your heart, and with fasting, and with weeping and with mourning:"*

God has all the power you could ever need or ask for. He is a powerful God that saves. During the days of Joel as many destructions begin to turn their world upside down, Joel believed greater in the

<u>God ALMIGHTY has been waiting on you to arrive.</u>
powers of God. He knew Him as a Savior. If you take a good look at your life, notice the many things that have tried to destroy you. Many times, war was all around you, but God brought you out. You cannot let the things around you stop you from fighting this battle. You must be prepared to fight back and prepared to win this war. It is time to fight for your life; your future is depending on it. Use all that God has given you and rise up. The sooner you rise up He will draw everything to you that you will ever need to be an overcomer. No, you cannot possibly make such a move on your own, but you can make it with the power of God. Sincerity must overtake your heart so; therefore, God can place a new charge in your life. Use The Anointing Powers in your hands. He has the power to destroy all destruction around you. Just lay your hands on it. Do not worry about how you are going to get it done just know in your heart that God is going to do it. Look at your hands and see their worth. Look in the mirror and see God in you. I tell people if you cannot notice God in you then get Him to come into your heart. Let Him grow larger in you and get to know His Anointing Powers. After all, the larger He grows in you, the stronger you will become. You will be more powerful because you will be teaming up with Heaven. God will save you in the nick of time once you repent. Anyone that calls upon Him shall be saved and shall be delivered. They shall obtain His Anointing Powers. His powers will work

<u>*God ALMIGHTY has been waiting on you to arrive.*</u>
through you all-powerfully. When you really want a miracle to happen in your life you will give God what He wants from you. You will give Him your heart; you will repent and you will get to know Him in a powerful manner. *Joel 2:13 says, "And rend your heart and not your garments, and turn unto the Lord your God for he is gracious and merciful, slow to anger, and of great kindness, and repenteth him of the evil."*

Notice that every time you repent you allow God to take charge of your life. It commissions Him to have full control and He rids your life of the evilness. In order for you to fight a war, you must be fully equipped with all the heavenly ammunition you will ever need to win. Yes, Heaven will be your ammunition and nothing has the power to destroy like Heavenly Powers. Fighting a war is serious and nothing to play around with. There are many different techniques you must understand, many ways to battle in order to defeat your enemy. However, know with the power of God you will win. Be prepared to come out as the winner. Once your enemy realizes the power that you have working on the inside of you he will flee with no thought of return. God has the power to make you defeat every stronghold, enemy, bound up situation and anything that has held you back from your life promises. You need Him now more than ever working in your life. Use what He has given you to

God ALMIGHTY has been waiting on you to arrive.
win. Your faith is your weapon to defeat every enemy in your life. You must keep your mind focused on those blessed promises; your future depends on it. Understand only God has the power to bring rejoicing. God will intervene in your life, once you know Him. Many people fail to realize how blessed they really are, just lay your hands on it. He will even cause you to rejoice in your wartime because in your heart you know that you will not be defeated. Do you want to rejoice in your heart forever or want your land to overflow with milk and honey? Only one winner comes out of every war so therefore be prepared to fight until you win. *Psalms 104:34 says, "My meditation shall be sweet: I will be glad in the Lord."*

There was many times in my life I did not want to go forth. I had no motivation, because my heart was not in Him. The day I stopped allowing everything in my life to be held back is the day I began to move ahead. When I set my mind on the powers of God then God gave me a way out. God has given all of us an opportunity to overcome our life's devastations. No one can move until his or her heart is made up. As He showed me my future, the things that could appear and the way He had purposed me to live, I realized I had to do better. Not only did I want to do better but also, my heart desired to live in His Eternal Blessings. I had to ask the Lord for forgiveness. I knew He had given me

God ALMIGHTY has been waiting on you to arrive.

great gifts but they could not do my life any good until I wanted Him. I wanted things in my life so badly to change until I could taste it. I tasted His sweetness. I was not ready to truly trust God that it could happen in my life. Though I tried many things such as praying, going to church, studying His word, getting to know Him, I still had to meditate on His goodness. As I begin a life of meditation with the Lord, He began to give me power. He took me out of self and allowed me to feel His presence. Meditating on His goodness will get you where you need to be in life. You must understand some things that God wants from you. God has the power to give you purchasing power. I mean when you need something it will be available for you to get it. When you meditate, you become focused. In addition, once you are in His presence you will have the power to do anything you need to do. In order to become an achiever you must first know one. Though you may think you know Him, get to know Him in a greater manner. I knew in my heart it was time for me to live in my land flowing with milk and honey. Do you feel that way sometimes, you want it to be your time? Have faith you can achieve whatever He has called you to do and then it will be your time. God planned for you to get to know Him. You must expect it to be your time. I mean everything you ever hoped for and your heart ever desired. Meditate on Him through the good and the bad. Oh, I really have had many bad things happen

God ALMIGHTY has been waiting on you to arrive.

in my life. In addition, when things grew worst I meditated more on His word. It brought me through every bad situation.

Oftentimes, people are too comfortable in their lives. However, when things are good in their lives, are they where God would have them to be? Yes, some have a good life as you look from the outside in but is it pleasing to God? If there is a lack in your life then you are not where God wants you to be. *Psalms 104:34 says, "My meditation shall be sweet: I will be glad in the Lord."*

As I think of His goodness, my heart is satisfied in Him. Though times I too doubted Him, I grew to trust Him. In addition, as I lacked many things in my life, struggled more than often I grew to need Him more. I realized God did not create me to live a life of lack; He wanted my life to be supplied with every need. Nevertheless, I lived in doubt through my dis-obedience that caused my life to lack the way it did. As I lacked my children suffered and many other things we had to live without. My husband lived under many life pressures and my visions stayed buried. Lack will put a tremendous strain on your prosperity and it will keep you living in stress. Now that I know Him, I trust Him with my life. He will turn your life around. As I think of His goodness my soul says, "Hallelujah!" as my heart is filled with joy. I owe

God ALMIGHTY has been waiting on you to arrive.
Him all the credit because without Him I could have done nothing. He simply did it all and I give Him the Glory. He is my Precious Father and my Teacher. He has instructed me to have faith and He is my Personal Savior. I adore His sweetness and I will forever need Him to be the instructor of my life. He is my Life Instructor. Have faith that you can achieve and then you will. *Joel 3:10 says, Beat your plowshares into swords, and your pruning hooks into spears: let the weak say, I am strong.*

    Once you realize that you need the power of God to accomplish this work, it will be done. Your heart will begin to desire a greater work and your usual work will cease. Step out of self and step into the powers of God. Your faith must walk for you. Only God can cause such a miraculous change in your life and you must desire Him in your heart. You must be willing to be changed from the inside out. Before I was weak, and I had no strength. Once I begin to meditate on God's goodness I refused to let anything stop me from making it. I kept all those wonderful promises God told me. I had a purpose to move forward and to aim for greatness. Be determined to make it over and you will overcome. Every time you move forward, you will move closer to God's promises. I was not going to let no enemy, no sin or a life struggle stop me from making it through. Sometimes we are so busy holding on to things and people until often times we lose our

God ALMIGHTY has been waiting on you to arrive.
connection with God. Often times we hold on to things that God wants us to let go.

Building your Trust in Jesus to Live Your Dreams

- *Your doubt must be consumed by putting your trust in Him.*
- *You must Move Closer to Jesus in order to be in Him and for Him to live in you.*
- *Do Not Let Anything Stop You.*
- *Get Spiritually Motivated In a church and take part in the service.*
- *Never sit down and fall asleep on the word you will only dream your life away.*
- *Attend at least 2 worship services a week to be fed a true word of life.*
- *Set aside a designated time, relax your mind and focus in on His Powers. Let God feed your mind power.*
- *Make sure you find a quiet resting place and meditate daily.*
- *Always read a scripture before you meditate, the word will feed your life. You can meditate on the same scripture until it soak into your heart.*
- *Log your daily meditation in your agenda make it a daily priority.*

Meditation relaxes the mind. It connects you with greater power as it soothes your soul. It will

<u>*God ALMIGHTY has been waiting on you to arrive.*</u> attach you to a world not of your own, as it will deepen your trust in Him. Meditate on His goodness, surely taste His sweetness. Get comfortable in Him; listen as He speaks to you. He will cause your troubles to go away. Constantly speak life to yourself and never accept the bad things that will come against you, just focus in on the good. Just because you have not made it yet, know that it is coming. Remember, every runner has their time to get to the finish line. Some run faster, others a little slower. Nevertheless, keep in mind if you quit you will never make it to the finish line. So, keep on journeying in your vision. Keep running and eventually you will get there. Continue writing your vision. Plan to live your dreams.

Fighting For What You Want

- *Get a plan together – Get prepared*
- *It is your vision, your land where are your goals? Write your goals down & get a strategy.*
- *You must know where you are going in life.*
- *Write your plan down and do your research.*
- *Study your plan and then revise it as more develop.*
- *Let your meditation time grow, it is time to double it. In addition, open up to God*

<u>God ALMIGHTY has been waiting on you to arrive.</u>
more in prayer. Gas yourself up in your prayer power.

- *Add a few bible studies to your agenda monthly. Spiritual increase is like exercising, it takes time. The more you work on it the more spiritually fit you will become. Remember, your action to move towards Him causes Him to respond to you.*

Vision:

Vision is *something* that takes time and plenty of preparation. The greater effort you put in preparing your vision the sooner it will come forth. Write a strong vision and do not rush it. Do all your necessary foot work and research. Plan it out to the tee. It took me years to write my visions. Use every resource you can and then get to know your vision. Visions are personal because they come from within the heart. The more you prepare it the sooner you will want it and the more your heart is going to desire it. After you have fully prepared your vision, now it is time to make any changes. Revise it, which simply means you are proofing it. As you add and then make changes begin studying your vision. It needs to be fully together. Place it in front of you; keep it at your fingertips. Do not depend on anyone to help you other than God. Add your

God ALMIGHTY has been waiting on you to arrive.

vision to your meditation time with God. Fast over your vision and allow God to consecrate it. God has the power to raise anything up from the dead. He will give your vision life and it will speak. Be patient as God begins to prepare you to handle receiving it. He works at His pace and not yours. Daily continue in these quick notes, keep putting your hands on it. God is going to anoint the work of your hands. Get ready to face the TRUTH for the victory is in your hands.

- *Write down the blessings you want to give.*
- *Write down how your vision is going to please God.*
- *Write down how much you have progressed.*
- *Keep a to-do list for your vision, making the steps.*
- *Know the purpose of your vision.*
- *Bless in seven ways within the next 30 days.*

The Purpose of your vision:

It should be *to* bless someone with love, giving from your heart and helping another up. Often times we do not receive our blessings because our hearts are not where God would have them to be. Many people just do not know how to show love. Prove to God that you have a good heart and start

God ALMIGHTY has been waiting on you to arrive.

practicing living it. The more you begin to be a blessing the sooner God is going to bless you. Begin sowing goodness and needed blessings to other people. Listen to their needs and let God lead you to be a blessing to them. Be prepared for more doors to open on your behalf. When we bless with love God blesses us. Perhaps buy someone flowers that are not expecting it. Treat someone to dinner that needs to go somewhere. Buy someone a gift card and mail it to him or her. However, as God blesses you to be a blessing you will receive more. By a friend a new outfit just because. So many wait until Christmas to give gifts but it should be a year round thing. God wants us to be more of a blessing, spread love, joy and cause someone to want to smile. Do from your heart and watch God work. Hold no grudges in your heart; let it be filled with love. Watch Him work more in your life. If you sow more love, you will receive greater love in your life. I tell many to sow what you need and let God increase you. We all want to be loved, after all God is love. Live every day to be merry, live in love.

Your spiritual development is the most important thing right now. Treat it as though your life depends on it because it does. In your worship service, get involved. Stay

<u>*God ALMIGHTY has been waiting on you to arrive.*</u>
focused on the word and take it all in. Practice it and see it come to light. You must stay inspired, as you are aiming to reach the height of your vision. Do not give up it will all come to pass and fight harder.

- *Prayer will get you to the source of your power.*
- *The key unlocks your needs.*
- *Treat prayer as though it is your lifeline because through it you receive powerful support.*
- *Take your time and pray more.*
- *Designate your prayer time with God.*
- *Get more into it with your heart.*
- *Let nothing interrupt your prayer life.*
- *Never stop praying, no matter what.*

Prayer:

- Prayer is your power and it will open the doors for The Spirit of God to commune with you. The Spirit will feed you spiritually. It will strengthen you with Heavenly Powers and it will give you the power to overcome anything. Prayer empowers you. Do not live without it. By now, you should have noticed a spiritual change within your life. You should be receiving more power. Your vision should have a form and your motivational level in it

God ALMIGHTY has been waiting on you to arrive.
should be increased. Perhaps, if not, go back and study your quick notes. Follow the instructions before you go further in this book. It is all right to start over especially when it is going to serve a life changing difference.

- For the ones that have seen movement and have been encouraged in their visions, you are on your way. Continue in these quick notes as you continue to read. If a certain quick note moved more in your life then try it again. Remember, everything you learn continue it especially when you see it working in your life.

- As you continue to read this book, it is time for you to go to the next level. Yes, you are graduating. Notice as you spiritual graduate your vision will also increase.

   1. Begin your blessing technique again.
   2. Bless as many as God would have you in the next seven days of your life.
   3. Work on speaking more to people; help lift their spirits by just giving someone a compliment.
   4. Share a word of encouragement with someone for the next week of your life.

<u>God ALMIGHTY has been waiting on you to arrive.</u>

5. Smile everywhere you go.
6. Sow a seed for the prosperity of your vision. Let God move you on where to sow your seed. Make it one that is going to be large enough to cause your vision to come forth sooner.
7. Pray over everything you do like never before and tell God what you want from every good deed and seed you sow.

Prayer:

- Prayer gives us power and power causes us to love. Love moves mountains and it clears our way. As we walk in love, blessings follow and as we sow good seeds, God returns them to us. Watch as you pray and expect many good things to come your way. God lives through His people and a person receives God through us. Show greater love in your heart for people and God will show that His love is great in your life.

- Make sure after following these quick notes to please write me and share your testimonies, I would love to share them with others. Please read the testimony insert in the back of the book.

<u>God ALMIGHTY has been waiting on you to arrive.</u>

You Should Never Walk By Sight

- *No matter what your eyes see always expect a miracle.*
- *When things get rough for you, feed yourself more of Jesus any way possible.*
- *When giants appear never look at them, see GOD.*
- *When you begin to feel the pressures of life, sing a good old time spiritual song, pump your spirit up.*
- *Do not share all your vision plans with every one, some will not want to accept them.*
- *Do what you have to do to keep your faith growing.*

<u>More Divine Books by Parker C Parker</u>

The Anointing Power of your Hands

Powerful Inspiring books by Parice Parker

Living Life in A Messed Up Situation

Volume One

Living Life in A Messed Up Situation

Volume Two

Aggravated Assault on Your Mind

A Precious Gift from God

Word Wonders

The Anointing Powers of Your Hands

From Eating Crumbs to Transforming Wealth

The Birth of an Author Shall Be Born

Live Love Laugh & Be Happy

Breaking the Back of Poverty

Breaking the Back of Poverty the Journal

Visit Our Online Book Store or Where Ever Books Are Sold
www.pariceparker.biz or www.pariceparker.org

More Divine Books by Parker C Parker

Aggravated Assault on Your Mind

Have you ever felt, the very person you have surely loved or believed in has attacked you? It may have been your closest friend, relative, child, your spouse or even yourself. Sometimes you wanted to cry and could not. Shortly afterwards, while gazing about the pain immediately tears began to fall as a flowing river. Your heart has been

More Divine Books by Parker C Parker

assaulted and snared with claws of intentions to kill. A multitude of thoughts circulate in your mind and then you began to say to yourself **"How did I let this happen to me?"** Your situation was bound to occur, because somewhere along the way you have allowed your circumstance to control your mind. Allegedly, you put your trust in the wrong one or thing and then you are thrown off guard. Most definitely, you wonder, who do I blame? You did not realize you have entrusted so much of your heart to be assaulted through the passion of love you have given. A since of blindness has overwhelmed your thinking ability, rearranging your life, and throwing it off balance. Truly, there is an explanation and an apology due, but none is ever given. Certainly, you have tried to generate an effectual change. Perhaps, the more you have tried, the more your relationship seemed to die. **Instantly thinking, What Is The Use?**

More Divine Books by Parker C Parker

A Precious Gift from God

Your Gift Discovery? It teaches one the value of their natural born talent and motivates one to Live Life On Purpose! This book inspires the heart, gives courage to your *How to Ability* and causes you to live in the pursuit of your happiness. Every natural born leader needs to read this book, it is **AWE – INSPIRING!**

More Divine Books by Parker C Parker

Living Life In A Messed Up Situation
Volume One

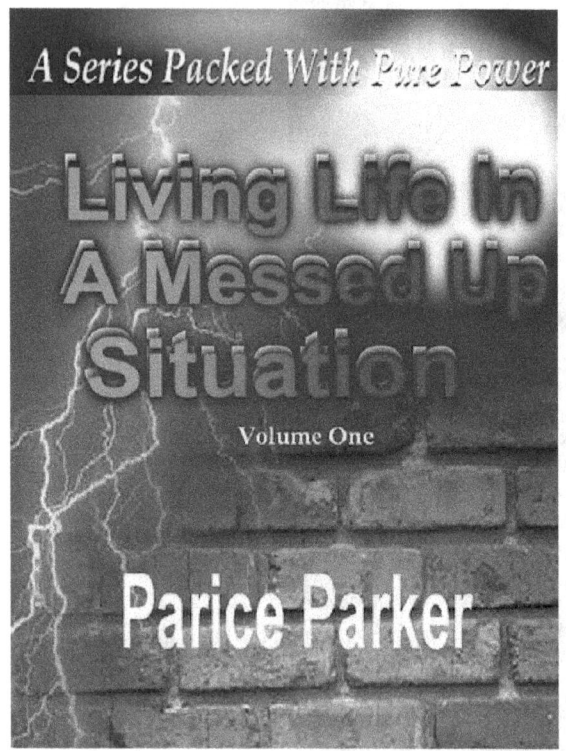

God will assign the most in-depth spiritual cleaning service through the Blood of Jesus the Christ to clean up your messed up life. **Every messed up situation that you are living** in will have a **Sparkling Effect** when God gets finished with you. Some things He dusts off, others He wipes down and some need to be polished to shine. **Get Polished Perfect** after reading this book and simply gain it all.

More Divine Books by Parker C Parker

Living Life In A Messed Up Situation
Volume Two

Astounding ... It seems though many things has changed within your life including your perseverance. Often you wanted to quit but couldn't afford to even STOP TRYING! As life twirled down so did your hope, dreams and prosperity. Order this book today and Reel In Your Greatest CATCH! A Mega Booster is what you need and this is it! Let JESUS catch You Trying!

More Divine Books by Parker C Parker

The Birth of An Author Shall Be Born

Fascinating ... Dazing at the fact you have a book inside and don't know where to start or how to get it out! This book have dynamic key points and great strategies on how to succeed in book writing from start to finish. It's time to discover the author in you and to **GET THAT BOOK OUT Of YOU!** This book is full of techniques to motivate the author inside... The Birth of an Author Shall Be Born, Is It YOU?

More Divine Books by Parker C Parker

Word Wonders

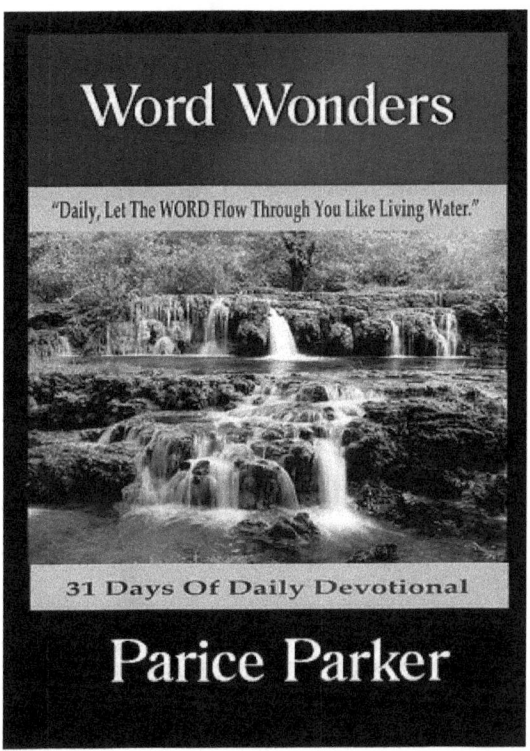

A Eye – Opening ... Word Wonder inspires your HOPE to Greatly Influence your FAITH and it's a magnificent daily devotional book to help keep you focused in word. It EMPOWERS Positive Powers to cause DIVINE FAVOR to ABOUND TOWARDS YOU! Simple things you need to be equipped with more favor from on high. Get This Book TODAY!

More Divine Books by Parker C Parker

From Eating Crumbs To Transforming Wealth

Riveting ... Finally, a book that keeps you in a thriving mental state that causes your HOPE to burst through! Now, it is time to identify the real you by introducing the TROPHY that is Hidden inside. It's your time to stop eating the crumbs of life and Indulge In Your WEALTHY Place!

More Divine Books by Parker C Parker

Live Love Laugh & Be Happy

Live Love Laugh & Be Happy *Fabulous* ... Daily many live life being terribly unhappy wanting others to really care but, are too often overlooked. It's time you get a new ray of hope. A time for healing inside and out. Live Love Laugh & Be Happy is purposed to expose new life to your everyday living. Your laughter is on its way, because those that sow in tears of sorrow, shall reap in tears of joy!

More Divine Books by Parker C Parker
Thanks You So Much & Be Blessed!

Parice C. Parker

How does one define a powerhouse of excellence? Is this achieved by the sheer magnitude of what survey would describe excellence is? We know that survey is oftentimes fickle and led to fluctuations. And, just how do we measure the power in a powerhouse?

More Divine Books by Parker C Parker

It seemed a simple enough inquiry, didn't it? Well, it's not, especially when it comes to the matter of Parice Parker, Apostle, Visionary, and One Who Simply Defies and while mystifying what a very limited survey deems appropriate for one such as Parice.

Successful Business Owner/Entrepreneur in her 20s of one of the most prestigious hair emporiums in the Queen City (aka Charlotte, NC) before hair matters became vogue!

Author and Publisher Extraordinaire to the masses for Christian Reality & Christian Fiction through her enterprise Fountain of Life Publisher's House. Visionary to bring that which is hidden in plain sight to the fore!

Parice Parker, Apostle of the liberated and undefeated champions who dare to go beyond the limited and restrictive situations in their life to live a life of power.

Apostle Parker has broken every chain when it comes to her overall health matters. Not merely a stroke survivor, a Champion of 10 Strokes, which should have killed her instantly. She because of her Faith in the Power that resides within her has moved against the dark portals of disability. She is enabled to surely move mountains with a force that is truly inspiring.

More Divine Books by Parker C Parker

Parice Parker your next hope for elevation in situations where survey deems it all done and over. But, oh this is so not the case. Please visit: www.pariceparker.org or www.thehotatl.org or www.pariceparker.biz to find out more as to why you need to hear from her for yourself!

More Divine Books by Parker C Parker